The Independent
Record Label's

GUIDE TO

CONTRACTING

The Independent Record Label's

PLAIN & SIMPLE

GUIDE TO

CONTRACTING

SHAWNASSEY HOWELL BRITT

iUniverse, Inc.
New York Lincoln Shanghai

The Independent Record Label's Plain and Simple
Guide to Contracting

iUniverse books may be ordered through booksellers or by contacting:

iUniverse
2021 Pine Lake Road, Suite 100
Lincoln, NE 68512
www.iuniverse.com
1-800-Authors (1-800-288-4677)

Editor: Mary Jacq Easley
Cover Design: Lauren Cavadel

First Printing, 2004
Second Printing, 2005

ISBN-13: 978-0-595-31129-3 (pbk)
ISBN-13: 978-0-595-75957-6 (ebk)
ISBN-10: 0-595-31129-6 (pbk)
ISBN-10: 0-595-75957-2 (ebk)

Printed in the United States of America

Acknowledgements

Many people have assisted in this project, and I hope that everyone involved realizes how much I appreciate their help and enthusiasm. Thanks to Mary Jacq Easley and Lauren Cavadel for generously sharing their expertise and limited time, to Mike Frascogna, Brenda Marsalis, Anita Campbell and everyone else at the firm for their guidance, perspective and assistance, and to all of the clients, for showing me the practical side of the record business.

Contents

PART ONE

RECORDING AGREEMENTS

Introduction

More and more, enterprising people are striking out on their own to form and operate independent record labels. Considering the turmoil currently being experienced by the major labels, the landscape is friendlier to the independent label than it ever has been before, especially with the advent of the Internet and its unprecedented ability to offer products worldwide at minimal cost.

However, many people form a label with just a dream. Although dreams are the inspiration for many great things, it takes more than a dream to run a business. It takes hard work, organization, planning, financing, marketing and, most importantly from this book's standpoint, concrete understandings between everyone involved in the venture. That is, unfortunately, one of the areas that gets lost in the shuffle. Record label heads are seldom at a loss for eager artists, and frequently understand the importance of funding and marketing. However, too many times record companies rely on handshake deals (or worse yet, on no deal at all), instead of taking the time to hammer out detailed arrangements and get written commitments. In fact, we spend a substantial amount of time dealing with people whose gentlemen's agreement turned bad when sales begin to generate money.

Although *it is always advisable to consult an attorney to negotiate and prepare any contracts that you might need*, this book provides a detailed explanation of the contracts used by record labels, complete with examples based on real life experiences. Take the time to do it right. Your success depends on it.

Chapter 1

So You've Discovered the Next Sensation

Although there is an abundance of talented artists with the desire to "make it big," finding an artist that has the special spark that will catch the public's attention is no easy task. In fact, with major and independent labels alike, for every band on their label that is successful (assuming there is one) there are easily half a dozen that aren't.

But once you've found the artist that you think can make things happen and you've made the decision to enter into a business relationship with each other, what happens next?

The record deal.

Recording Artist Agreements

Recording artist agreements come in all shapes and sizes, depending on the points that are most important to you. From the 50-page nightmares used by large record labels to the fairly simple 2-page deals that may be used by fledgling independent labels, these agreements can vary widely in form and content. However, understanding that we could never show you every variation of recording agreement, here are some very standard terms that you should consider for your agreement.

A. Term

The term of the agreement is a fairly simple concept—it is the length of the contract. Before you get too comfortable with that explanation, however, you should understand that the "Term" is almost never a straight number of years. Here is a sample "Term" provision:

a. *The term hereof (the "Term") shall consist of an initial period (the "First Contract Period) plus the additional "Contract Periods", if any, by which such Term may be extended by Company's exercise of one or more of the options granted to Company below (unless otherwise extended or suspended as provided herein).*

b. *You hereby irrevocably grant to Company two (2) consecutive options to extend the term for a Contract period. The Company may exercise its option by giving you notice at any time prior to the date that the then current Contract Period would otherwise expire.*

c. *The First Contract Period shall commence on the date hereof and each Contract Period shall continue until the date twelve (12) months after the Delivery to the Company of the Minimum Recording Commitment for such Contract Period.*

d. *Notwithstanding anything to the contrary contained in this agreement, if the first Album recorded and released for the initial Contract Period fails to achieve USNRC Net Sales in excess of Fifty Thousand (50,000) units (as reported by SoundScan) as of the date nine (9) months after its initial United States retail street date (the "Street Date"), the Company may at any time up to and including the thirtieth (30th) day after the Street Date terminate the term of this agreement by written notice to you, in which event all parties will be deemed to have fulfilled all of their obligations hereunder (except those that survive the term hereof).*

As you can see, the term may be expressed as releases, rather than years (in fact, most record companies do it that way because it gives them some flexibility with their release schedule). The term may extend until a period of months after the album's "street date" (that is, the date that the album is officially released) or after "delivery" of the album (that is, when the master recordings are completed and delivered to the record company). For instance, a fictional pop band, Groove Therapy, catches the ear of Livin' Large Records, which wants to sign Groove Therapy to an exclusive recording artist contract. Livin' Large will likely give the group an "initial term" that equals one album. If Livin' Large's contract is measured by the album's street date, the initial term will begin on the day Groove Therapy signs the contract and will end, for instance, nine months after the album's commercial release.

However a record company chooses to express the initial term, the record company should reserve several one-sided options to renew the contract if it decides the album is selling well enough to merit another release. In fact, as shown here, many record companies will include a clause that will terminate the contract if a certain level of sales is not achieved within the first nine months to one year. Therefore, if Groove Therapy's first album goes platinum, chances are, Livin' Large will exercise its first option and require the group to record another album. On the other hand, if sales of the album are nominal, Livin' Large may allow the contract to terminate at the end of the initial term. Keep in mind that these options are always on the record company's side, and if Groove Therapy does not agree with Livin' Large's decision to go forward with another album (or not to), Groove Therapy is out of luck.

Biz Note: Generally, the first term will be for a single album and there will be anywhere from 3 to 5 additional options (and the options are usually counted when you're referring to the number of albums in the deal—if you offer your artist a "four album deal," what you're offering is one firm album and three options). But watch out! The contract will either have the options renew automatically or have you send a written notice of renewal. Either choice has its downside—if you forget to stop an automatic renewal, you could find yourself obligated to record and release (and more to the point, pay for) an album for a non-profitable group. On the other hand, if you forget to send a notice for a manual renewal, you could lose your options on a band that has good income potential.

B. Territory

The Territory of the contract means the places in which the contract is effective, usually "the world" or, when a record company has a particularly compulsive lawyer, "the universe." You should not limit the contract to the country that your artist lives in. Artist's services are valuable everywhere, and you will want the option to release the works, and limit the artist's right to record for other record companies, worldwide. Of course, you won't be obligated to exploit the record worldwide, but you will at least have that option. Territory provisions are usually fairly concise:

> *The territory covered hereby (the "Territory") shall be the entire world.*

C. Services

The "Services" section describes what the record company will expect from the artist. This is the place where the record company will claim the artist's exclusive services. Any attempt to record for any other company during the term of the contract would be a breach of the agreement, unless the record company is willing to sign a waiver, called a side artist agreement, which will be discussed in chapter 6.

> *During the Term of the Agreement, you shall render to Company your exclusive services as a recording artist for the purpose of making Master Recordings in the Territory and as otherwise set forth herein.*

Many contracts will make exceptions for the artist's right to act as a producer for another artist, and will exclude other non-musical performances, such as television and movie appearances.

> *Notwithstanding anything to the contrary contained herein, nothing in this agreement is intended to prohibit Artist from rendering a non-musical performance in theatrical motion pictures or television productions and from granting home video rights to third persons with respect to such performances. Nothing herein is intended to prohibit you from performing customary producing services and receiving customary credit (without use of your likeness) as an independent producer in connection with Recordings of other artists.*

D. Recording Commitment

The recording commitment outlines how much product the record company will expect from the artist. Usually, the artist is expected to record one album containing newly recorded material per contract period, with the contract defining how many minutes of playing time constitutes an album.

However, you should reserve the right to add additional recordings to the commitment. For instance, our fictional record company, Livin' Large, decides to release a "tribute" album, paying homage to one of its artists that was recently killed in a car accident. Due to the enormous popularity of Groove Therapy's first album, released three months ago, Livin' Large may ask Groove Therapy to record a single song (a "side") for inclusion on the tribute album. The clause that allows the addition of recordings to a commitment provides for contingencies just such as this.

Most contracts will limit that right to one additional full album per contract year. You should also except special albums, such as Christmas albums, live albums, and so-called "Greatest Hits" albums from the recording commitment. Therefore, if the contract has these exceptions and the band compiles a "Greatest Hits" album for release, they still will have to record a regular album in order to fulfill the contract.

> *During each Contract Period, you shall render your services to Company, in accordance with the terms and conditions hereof, in connection with the recording of sides sufficient to constitute one (1) long playing album (the "Minimum Recording Commitment") of not less than forty-five (45) minutes. The Minimum Recording Commitment for each period shall be Delivered, as defined herein, to Company within six (6) months following the commencement of the applicable contract period, unless Company, at its sole and absolute discretion, extends the period for Delivery as required or desired by Company.*
>
> *Company shall have the right to increase your recording commitment in respect to any Contract Year; and you shall render to Company your exclusive services as a recording artist in connection with such additional number of Sides in excess of the Minimum Recording Commitment as Company may request from time to time. However, you shall not be obligated to perform hereunder for the recording of more than two (2) Albums (in the aggregate) during each Contract Year.*
>
> *Company may elect to release one or more so-called "Best Of," or "Greatest Hits" Albums and such Albums shall not reduce your Minimum Recording Commitment hereunder. With respect to each Greatest Hits Album scheduled for initial release during the term hereof, you agree to Deliver to Company, at Company's request and expense, two (2) newly recorded Masters embodying your performances of two (2) compositions that have not been previously recorded or released.*

E. Recording Procedure

The recording procedure describes the process of recording the masters. It can be a highly detailed accounting of every facet of the recording procedure or a simple statement of where and when the recording will take place. For example, a plain statement describing the recording procedure might look something like this:

In connection with Master Recordings to be made hereunder the selection of dates of recording and studio where recording is to take place, including the cost of recording therein, shall be mutually determined by you and Company provided that in the event of any dispute regarding such matters, Company's decision shall control.

Each Master Recording made hereunder shall be subject to Company's approval as "Satisfactory" (as defined herein) for the manufacture and sale of Phonograph Records. As used herein, Master Recordings shall be deemed "Satisfactory" if they contain first class vocal performances of a style and quality consistent with your previous recordings, and if (to the extent controlled in whole or in part by you) they are technically satisfactory for the manufacture and sale of phonograph records therefrom.

Nothing contained in this Agreement shall obligate Company to permit the continuation of any recording session to be held in connection with Master Recordings hereunder, if Company reasonably anticipates that the Master Recordings being recorded will not be Satisfactory.

In this example, the record company allows the artist to have some input into the dates and location of the recording, although the record company does reserve the right to make the final decision.

The second provision in the above example requires the artist to deliver "quality" recordings. If an artist attempts to satisfy the recording commitment by submitting recordings that are either artistically or technically sub-standard, this clause allows the record company to reject masters that are inconsistent with previous works. For instance, say our hypothetical band Groove Therapy is going into the studio to record their second album. The first album was successful and Groove Therapy has been working to re-negotiate their contract with Livin' Large. Although the record company has granted some concessions, the band still believes they are being short-changed. Groove Therapy is less than enthusiastic about the sessions, thinking that they are only creating another album for Livin' Large to exploit at their expense, and delivers a shoddy performance. When Livin' Large hears the masters (assuming it doesn't stop the recording before the masters are complete), it may reject them as non-marketable. This leaves Groove Therapy in breach of its contract for failing to deliver its recording commitment (not to mention indebted to the record company for any monies expended on the recordings).

A more complicated "Recording Procedure" clause covers a lot of additional ground. Detailed provisions might cover procedures for establishing budgets, forms and documents to be completed and tendered with the masters, and engagement of producers (or use of company producers).

Procedures for establishing budgets

Record companies should not allow recording to commence until they have authorized a budget for the recordings. This is very important! Many independent labels make the mistake of proceeding without a budget—this is the equivalent of handing your artist a blank check with which to make its recording. With an authorized budget, the artist knows exactly how much money it has to work with and is on notice that it will have to personally pay for any excess costs. The procedures for authorizing budgets can vary, but generally, the artist will have to submit a budget within a few weeks before recording is to begin. If the company rejects the budget, the artist will need to revise it to suit the company and re-submit.

Once the budget is established, the record company will generally advance the recording costs as long as the project is under budget. The artist may not go over budget unless the artist expects to pay the overage out of his or her own pocket. Many times the company will reserve the right to stop the recording if the company believes the album will go over budget.

Biz note: This is one of the stickier subjects for most start up labels. Some labels want so much to please their artists, especially if the artist has true selling potential, that they cave in and allow the artist to spend whatever they like on the album. Not only does this cut into the album's profitability and rob the company of funds it could be using to market the album, this can seriously interfere with the label's cash flow, *even if the album is successful.* Money tends to be spent in large chunks, but comes back in the door in small trickles over several years, if at all. Remember, as well, that there is a delay of at least two to three months between a sale and the time that the money makes its way back to the record company. Don't overextend yourself with the idea that album sales will make up the difference.

Document submission

A detailed "Recording Procedures" clause might outline what documents the artist must gather from those who contribute to the album. I-9s, W-9s, and other tax forms may be addressed. If the documents are not turned in to the company within the required time frame, the company may reserve the right to pass on any late penalties to the artist.

Producers

The artist is usually responsible for engaging the producer. The agreement might outline how the producer's advance and/or royalties are to be paid. It may also make provision for use of a company producer. If the producer is a salaried employee of the record company, the artist might assume that he or she does not have to pay for the service. However, the agreement usually establishes how much of the producer's salary is to be allocated to the artist for the producer's services.

F. Recoupable Costs

Certain costs that a record company incurs in connection with an artist's album are recoupable from the artist's royalties—in fact, once you begin examining the list of costs that a record company can recoup, you may wonder if there is anything a record company *doesn't* recoup. Recording costs are always recoupable (there might be an exception out there somewhere, but we haven't found it yet). Those costs usually include producers, mixers, engineers, studio costs, back-up vocalists and musicians, travel expenses, and the like. In addition, money paid directly to the artist as an advance is recoupable. Monies paid to the artist to assist with tour expenses (known as "tour support") are recoupable. Expenses for creating music videos are usually recoupable against video royalties and at least partially against album royalties. Many record companies will recoup some or all promotional and/or marketing costs that are specifically attributable to the artist. This can have a profoundly negative effect on artist royalties. A popular band of my acquaintance sold multiple millions of albums and still owed its record company well over half a million dollars, due to the large amount of money spent promoting the album. As you will see below, it is fairly common for an artist to *never collect any artist royalties at all.*

Other items are usually not recoupable, such as manufacturing and packaging costs (although some record companies will recoup "excess" packaging costs under some circumstances), graphics and photography, and distribution costs. That is not to say these items are not deducted before determining what the artist's royalty will be—it simply means that the artist does not have to repay the record companies for those costs.

Basically, here's how it works. Returning to our above example, Groove Therapy is unhappy with the Livin' Large Records because Groove Therapy did not understand how the royalty calculations are made. As the numbers began to come in, they were dismayed to see that after selling nearly 250,000 albums, they still were not collecting any artist royalties. They knew that their artist advance and costs for producing the masters totaled around $450,000. They also knew that they would have to pay that back. However, they thought that 250,000 albums times the wholesale of $8.00 per compact disc, totaling $2,000,000, was more than enough to repay the costs. In fact, they reasoned, after deducting the $450,000 advance, there was still $1,550,000 left from which they should collect their 15% royalty. Thinking they were entitled to $232,500, they were stunned to learn that they were not entitled to any royalties at all.

The first mistake that Groove Therapy made was assuming that the advance would be deducted from the record company's gross income. They realized that Livin' Large was not collecting the retail price of the compact discs, but they forgot to account for the fact that, even after collecting only wholesale price, the record company would deduct manufacturing and distribution fees and packaging costs. Next, the record company deducted "reserves." Reserves are monies set aside to accommodate for returns from retailers. These costs reduced the price per album used to calculate royalties from $8.00 per compact disc to approximately $2.00 per compact disc. (Many record companies calculate royalties on retail, but the method is similar).

Groove Therapy was able to accept that part of the explanation fairly calmly—they understood that the expenses had to be paid, so all of that money wasn't really available to repay the advance. However, they still thought that, at $2.00 per compact disc and 250,000 record sales, their advance was now paid with $50,000 left over from which they could collect royalties. Livin' Large's statement showed that they still owed the record company $375,000. Their second mistake was in assuming that Livin' Large's entire profit would be applied to repaying the advance. In fact, the advance was repaid at the same rate as they would have collected royalties. So instead of applying the entire $2.00 profit per album toward the $450,000 advance, the record company only applied Groove Therapy's 15%, or about $0.30 per album. At that rate, Groove Therapy quickly realized that they would see no artist royalties until the album sold over 1.5 million copies, and that was before the record company started assessing them with the costs of promoting the album.

This is commonly how recoupable costs are figured into artist royalty calculations. That is why the issue of recoupable vs. non-recoupable is so important. The more costs the record company designates as recoupable, the more it will be able to look to the artist for repayment and the longer artist royalties will be delayed.

Company will pay all specifically approved Recording Costs in connection with Master Recordings made hereunder, all costs of all

*non-royalty instrumental, vocal and other personnel, and arrange-
ments and copying incurred by Company hereunder, and all other
amounts which are required to be paid by Company pursuant to any
applicable law or any collective bargaining agreement between
Company and any union representing persons who render services in
connection with Master Recordings made hereunder.*

*Except for Artist royalties payable hereunder, all amounts described
in this Section, plus all other amounts paid by Company representing
expenses incurred in connection with the making of Master Recordings
hereunder are herein sometimes called "Recording Costs" and shall
constitute Advances.*

*All packaging costs in excess of Company's then standard design,
engraving or manufacturing costs with respect to a standard Record
package are recoupable from all monies payable to you hereunder.
Promptly after your written request therefore (which request may be
sent to Company, if at all, within ten (10) days after Company makes
the artwork for the Album available to you or your representatives),
Company will notify you if it anticipates incurring any such excess
design, engraving or manufacturing costs in connection with any
Album package hereunder. Provided that changing the Album package
would not unreasonably delay the scheduled release of the Record concerned, if you object to such excess design, engraving or manufacturing
costs in connection with an Album package not prepared by you or not
prepared at your request, and such written objection is received by
Company within five (5) days after Company's notice is issued to you,
and Company nevertheless uses such package, Company will not charge
you for the excess. No failure to so notify you will be deemed a breach
hereof provided that if Company fails to so notify you, Company will
not charge you for any such excess.*

Biz Note: This is why artist royalty percentages are a good negotiating tool. If
you're recouping all advances, production and promotional expenses and the
artist won't recoup anyway, it doesn't hurt the record company to give away an
extra percentage point or two (royalty percentages are called "points"). The
extra points usually mean the unrecouped balance will be a smaller amount,
not that the artists will recoup and begin to collect royalties.

G. Advances

In addition to recording costs, any other money paid to an artist under a recording artist contract is considered an "Advance." Record companies approach advances in a couple of different ways. Larger record labels tend to establish a budget, set a "recording fund" that is in excess of the budget by a fair amount, then expect all recording costs to be paid from the fund, with the artists retaining whatever is left.

For instance, continuing with our example, Livin' Large had established a recording fund for Groove Therapy's first album of $450,000. Livin' Large allowed the band members to take $100,000 as advance when the contract was signed, to use for their own purposes. The members of Groove Therapy had to quit their jobs to go on tour in support of the first album, so they needed the money to pay expenses until they started making money from the tour, the songwriting and publishing (which we'll discuss later), and album itself. Livin' Large set the remaining $350,000 aside to cover recording costs. They had established a budget of $350,000 for the album, but costs totaled only $275,000. Therefore, Livin' Large had $75,000 left, which it gave to Groove Therapy as an additional advance after the masters were delivered (if the project had been over budget—say $400,000—then Livin' Large could have forced Groove Therapy to pay the additional $50,000). Groove Therapy, then, divided a total of $175,000 among themselves, but their advance was the entire $450,000 recording fund.

As we discussed above, Livin' Large was still recouping artist royalties well beyond the point where Groove Therapy thought they should have been. However, you can see that Groove Therapy got some benefits on the front end. Had Groove Therapy decided to forgo the $175,000 cash payment before the album was released, they might have started collecting royalties sooner (although, with the moving target of promotional expenses assessed to the band, this is not likely). However, they would have had very little money to pay personal expenses with in the meantime.

Smaller labels often approach the issue of advances differently. Although many independent labels are able to make a comfortable amount of sales, smaller labels frequently do not achieve the level of sales that would allow them to recoup the recording costs from their projects. Therefore, many independent labels will pay recording costs directly as they occur and will pay the artist a smaller cash payment or none at all. On the other hand, artists that sign with smaller labels are less likely to tour to the point that it interferes with their livelihood, and large advances are not as critical.

A small label may approach the issue of advances like this:

> *In connection with the album Delivered in satisfaction of the Minimum Recording Commitment of the First Contract Period hereunder, Company agrees to pay you an advance recoupable from all royalties hereunder in the sum of Five Thousand Dollars ($5,000.00). Said Advance shall be payable 50% upon execution of this Agreement and 50% upon Delivery of the album.*
>
> *Any and all monies paid to you pursuant to this paragraph, as well as any and all other monies paid to you, or on your behalf, pursuant to or in connection with this Agreement (other than royalties), including Recording Costs, shall constitute Advances and shall be fully recoupable from Artist's royalties unless otherwise expressly agreed in writing by an authorized officer of Company.*

The agreement will frequently provide for advances for subsequent albums, if any are to be recorded:

> *In connection with the album Delivered in satisfaction of the Minimum Recording Commitment of the Second Contract Period hereunder, if any, Company agrees to pay you an advance recoupable from all royalties hereunder in the sum of Five Thousand Dollars ($5,000.00). Said Advance shall be payable 50% upon commencement of recording and 50% upon Delivery of the album.*

The agreement may also provide for advancing costs that are not directly related to the creation of the masters:

> *One-half (1/2) of all Video Costs will be recoupable from audio Record royalties. To the extent that any Video Costs are not recoupable or recouped from audio Record royalties, such costs will be recoupable from monies otherwise payable to you from the exploitation of videos hereunder. Fifty percent (50%) of all costs paid by Company to third parties in connection with independent marketing and/or independent promotion of Records featuring the performance of Artist will constitute Advances. All costs paid by Company in connection with "live" public Performances by Artist will constitute Advances.*

As you can see, although related costs may constitute advances, these costs may not be fully recoupable by the record company. Here, video costs are fully recoupable against the video itself, but only half of those costs can be recouped against the sale of albums. Any live performance costs paid by the record company are recoupable, but only half of the costs of the independent marketing is recoupable by the record company. These provisions can vary, but again, what is important is the concept of recoupable vs. non-recoupable. From the record company's perspective, you should ensure that as many costs as possible incurred on behalf of the artist may be recouped back from the artist's royalties.

Biz Note: Keep in mind that not "recouping costs" doesn't necessarily equal not making a profit. It simply means that the artist doesn't accrue enough royalties to pay the record company back for all of the expenses. For instance, in the example above, Groove Therapy still owes Livin' Large $375,000. However, after selling 250,000 units, even after deduction of its manufacturing and distribution costs, it is unlikely that the record company has actually lost money on the project.

H. Rights Granted

Recording contracts will generally outline in fair detail what rights the record company will have in any work product generated under the contract. These provisions usually state that the artist is providing its services on a "work for hire" basis and that all copyrights will belong to the record company. The record company will also want the right to use the artist's "name and likeness" in order to promote the album.

Keep in mind that copyrights to the masters should always belong to the record company, even though all of the costs are assessed against the artist (again, there might be an exception out there, but we have yet to find it). However, the copyrights are limited to the masters, and should not be general enough to encompass copyrights to the compositions themselves. An example of a provision that is written too broadly would be "all of your services hereunder shall constitute a work for hire." In this example "all of your services" could include songwriting if those services are addressed anywhere in the contract. If the record company intends to take a portion of the artist's publishing, there should be a separate provision for that, so that there is no dispute later on. Music publishing is a very important issue that we will address in more detail later.

All Master Recordings recorded hereunder from the inception of recording thereof, and all Phonograph Records manufactured therefrom, together with the performances embodied thereon, shall be the sole property of Company throughout the world, free from any claims whatsoever by you or any other Person; and Company shall have the exclusive right to copyright such Master Recordings in its name as the owner and author thereof and to secure any and all renewals and extensions of such copyright. Solely for the purposes of any applicable copyright law, all Persons rendering services in connection with the recording of such Master Recordings shall be deemed "employees for hire" of Company.

Without limiting the generality of the foregoing, Company and any Person authorized by Company shall have the unlimited right, throughout the world, to: manufacture Phonograph Records by any method now or hereafter known, derived from the Master Recordings made hereunder; to remix, edit or adapt the Masters to conform to technological or commercial requirements in various formats now or hereafter known or developed, or to eliminate material which might subject Company to any legal action; to sell, market, transfer or otherwise deal in the same under any trademarks, trade names and labels; and/or to refrain from any of the foregoing.

Company and any Person authorized by Company each shall have the right, and may grant to others the right, to reproduce, print, publish, or disseminate in any medium your name, portraits, pictures, likenesses and biographical material concerning you, as news or information, or for the purposes of trade, or for advertising purposes; provided, however, that no direct endorsement by you of any product or service shall be used without your prior written consent. During the Term of this Agreement, you shall not authorize any Party other than Company to use your name or likeness in connection with the advertising or sale of Phonograph Records. As used in this Agreement, "name" shall include any professional names or sobriquets.

I. Artist Royalties

Now we come to the core issue—just how much money is the record company going to pay the artist? As we explained above, artist royalties are not necessarily a gold mine to artists, mostly because of the recoupable costs that are assessed against artists. The royalty provisions will outline exactly what will be deducted, discounted and withheld before the artist's percentage, also set out in these provisions, is applied. Some record companies pay royalties based on wholesale price and some on retail. However, whether wholesale or retail is the starting point, the royalties are usually calculated in a similar manner. The record company will start with the relevant price and then will make adjustments for items such as packaging (frequently called a "container charge"), taxes, distribution costs, foreign sales, record club sales, promotional goods and returns.

Once all deductions are made, the record company will apply the artist's percentage to the net amount to come up with the artist's earned royalties. Then, the record company will deduct advances from the earned royalties to determine the amount actually payable to the artist. Until sales of the album are significant, there will usually be a negative balance on the artist's account that is carried forward into the next accounting period.

The artist's percentage will usually fall in the 10% to 18% range. The percentage varies based on a number of factors. Naturally, a multi-platinum recording artist will command a higher percentage than an unknown artist. Furthermore, the size of the label, the genre, and whether the percentage is based on wholesale or retail will have an impact on the percentage.

Royalty provisions are usually very detailed and are sometimes divided into several parts. As we noted, all of the deductions are outlined in these provisions. However, the deductions may not be clearly spelled out. They are frequently included by use of phrases that are defined elsewhere in the agreement. Therefore, as you will see, this is a way to camouflage the scope of the deductions by placing the actual deductions in an obscure place.

The following is a set of general royalty provisions, with explanations:

> *Conditioned upon your full and faithful performance of all the material terms and conditions hereof, you shall be paid in connection with the Net Sales of Records consisting entirely of Masters hereunder and sold by Company or its Licensees, a royalty computed as set forth hereinbelow:*

First of all, you should note that the Artist is paid on "net sales." Since the term is capitalized, the agreement should contain an explanation of what is deducted to arrive at the net sales figure (usually, there is a definition section that will define capitalized terms). In most cases, net sales will equal gross sales minus returns from retail outlets, credits and reserves. "Reserves" is a term used to represent a fund established in order to cover returns and credits. The record company will reserve the right to deduct a percentage of sales off the top and set it aside so that if a retail outlet returns items, there will be money to issue refunds. Some agreements will establish a cap on the percentage that may be deducted and some agreements will allow the company to deduct "reasonable" reserves, at its discretion:

> *Company shall have the right to withhold a portion of your royalties as a reserve for returns and/or credits, which reserve shall be determined by Company in its reasonable judgment.*

Reserves should be liquidated on a regular basis of anywhere from three months to one year. Therefore, if the reserve money remains unused, it is later credited back to the net sales figure.

Artist royalties generally appear fairly straightforward:

> *Fifteen Percent (15%) of the Royalty Base Price in connection with the Sale Through Normal Retail Channels in the United States of America of Phonograph Records in disc, tape, or other forms.*

You should again note that the percentage is of a defined term—Royalty Base Price. Therefore, the artist is not receiving 15% of retail or wholesale price. The artist receives 15% of another price, which is calculated by making the deductions such as packaging, taxes and distribution expenses. Again, the deductions are almost always set forth somewhere else in the agreement.

As you can see, there are reductions made as part of the term "Net Sales" (i.e. reserves and credits) and more reductions made as part of the term "Royalty Base Price." Further reductions are made as part of the next defined term, "Sale Through Normal Retail Channels." This means that sales that are not through normal retail channels will not have the same rate. In most cases, the agreement will specifically define what is not a sale through normal retail channels, and everything else will be considered a sale through normal retail channels. Similarly, this paragraph limits the 15% figure to United States sales, since the United States is where this particular record company operates. Therefore, if a sale under this contract occurs outside of the United States, another rate will apply.

If you are looking for additional ways to give the artist some concessions without breaking your pocketbook, you can offer an escalation of the artist's royalty rate. You can easily grant an increase as sales of the album increase, because greater volumes of sales generate enough income to make giving the extra fraction of a percent worthwhile. For instance, Groove Therapy's contract with Livin' Large might contain a 15% artist royalty rate for the first album until sales reached over half a million. If sales reach over half a million, the rate might increase to 15.5%, then to 16% if sales reach over one million and so forth. In addition, the contract may allow that the artist royalty rate for the second album start at the same rate that they achieved for the previous album. Therefore, if Groove Therapy ended up selling one million units of the first album, therefore achieving a rate of 16%, then for their next album, the base rate would start at 16% and would escalate from that point, depending upon sales.

Royalties are generally calculated differently for foreign sales:

> *In respect of Master Recordings licensed or made available by Company for the manufacture, distribution or sale of Phonograph Records through broadcast or other advertisement utilizing key-outlet distributors or any similar method of operation, or through any record club, mail order or similar operation or for use in connection with so-called "premium" operation or for use on a particular Record that is intended for sale through customary retail trade channels, or licenses of Masters on a flat fee or cent rate, Company shall credit your royalty account with fifty percent (50%) of the net royalty actually received by Company from such third parties after deducting all applicable third party payments.*
>
> *In respect of Phonograph Records sold and audio visual devices sold to educational institutions, libraries, to armed forces post exchanges, through television or telemarketing and in respect of Multiple Albums or Mid-Priced Records, the royalty payable to you shall be two-thirds (2/3) of the otherwise applicable royalty rate.*
>
> *In respect of Budget Records, the royalty rate payable to you shall be one-half (1/2) the otherwise applicable royalty rate.*

These are examples of sales that are not through normal channels. As you can see, the artist's royalty rate can be reduced by 1/3 to 1/2 for records sold at a discount. For record club sales, the artist's percentage does not apply, and the artist receives half of the record company's net royalty. This is a good place to note that the record company should *always* calculate based on net, not gross, receipts. Some record companies make the mistake of crediting the artist with a percentage of gross receipts. If the artist does recoup (which can happen, for instance, if the contract does not permit the record company to recoup promotional costs), this can result in the record company paying royalties based on income that the record company does not actually receive.

Another issue sometimes raised by recording artist agreements is the sale of albums in "new configurations":

> *With respect to compact discs, the royalty rate (which will be deemed to be the Basic Rate with respect to such configuration) is*

eighty two and one-half percent (82.5%) of the otherwise applicable royalty rate in the applicable country for the configuration and price category concerned. With respect to Records sold in the form of new configurations (including, but not limited to, Digital Compact Cassette, Mini Disc, Electronic Transmissions, and audiophile Records), the royalty rate (which will be deemed to be the Basic Rate with respect to such configurations) is seventy-five percent (75%) of the otherwise applicable royalty rate in the applicable country for the configuration and price category concerned.

Artist contracts typically provide for reduced royalties when an album is sold in a so-called new configuration, in order to account for the fact that new configurations are, initially at least, more expensive to manufacture. For example, years ago, the standard configurations for albums were vinyl records and cassettes. When compact discs came along, they were more expensive to manufacture than cassettes and records, so the record companies wanted the right to reduce the royalty rate in order to offset the extra expense. Compact discs have been on the market for long enough that they are no longer a "new configuration." However, as you can see, record companies may still reduce the base rate for compact discs. In the above example, there is a 17.5% reduction if the unit sold is a compact disc, rather than a cassette. Considering that most sales are in the form of compact discs, this provision effectively constitutes an across the board reduction in rates.

In respect of Phonograph Records sold by Company or its Licensees for distribution in Canada, or licensed or otherwise furnished by Company or its Licensees to others for its manufacture or distribution in Canada, the royalty rate payable to you therefor shall be eighty-five percent (85%) of the applicable basic royalty rate which would have been payable to you if such Records had been sold for distribution in the Untied States of America. In respect of Phonograph Records sold by Company or its Licensees for distribution in the United Kingdom, Italy, France, Germany, Australia or Japan, the royalty rate payable to you therefor shall be seventy-five percent (75%) of the applicable basic royalty rate which would have been payable to you if such Records had been sold for distribution in the Untied States of America. In respect of Phonograph Records sold by Company or its Licensees for distribution outside of the United States of America other than in Canada, the United Kingdom, Italy, France, Germany, Australia or Japan, or licensed or otherwise furnished by Company or its Licensees to others for its manufacture or distribution outside of the United States of America other than in Canada, the United Kingdom, Italy, France, Germany, Australia or Japan, the royalty rate payable to you therefor shall be one-half (1/2) of the applicable basic royalty rate which would have been payable to you if such Records had been sold for distribution in the Untied States of America.

This is an example of how foreign sales may be addressed. Here, sales in Canada would result in a 15% reduction of the artist's rate. Sales in the United Kingdom, Italy, France, Germany and Japan would result in a 25% reduction of the rate. Sales in non-named countries would result in a 50% reduction.

If Company licenses Videos or makes commercial use of such Videos embodying Artist's performances, the royalty payable by Company to you shall be one-half (1/2) of Company's net receipts derived therefrom after deducting any and all direct costs and/or third party payments in connection with the creation, manufacture, exploitation or use of the Videos from Artist's share of net receipts and an additional fee in lieu of any overhead or distribution of twenty-five percent (25%) of gross receipts. If any item of direct costs is attributable to receipts from such uses of Masters made hereunder and other master recordings, the amount of the expense item that will be deductible in computing the net receipts under this paragraph will be determined by apportionment.

With respect to home video devices embodying Artist's perform-ances, if Company manufactures and distributes such devices through its distributor, rather than licensing a third party to do so, the following shall apply: on units sold for distribution in the United States of America, fifteen percent (15%) of the Royalty Base Price; and on units sold for distribution outside the United States of America, ten percent (10%) of the Royalty Base Price. Said royalties shall be calculated after deducting any third party payments required in connection with the sale of such devices including, without limitation, artist and producer royalties and copyright payments.

As you can see, music videos are addressed separately from audio-only rates. Commercial use of videos by the record company generally results in a flat 50% of net receipts (minus a set overhead cost), to the artist. However, videos that are manufactured for home use carry a percentage similar to the album rate.

As we discussed briefly above, record companies may release compilation albums, or may release a master that contains the performances of more than one feature artist. When this occurs, the record company will generally pro-rate the artist's regular royalty rate.

Notwithstanding anything to the contrary contained herein:

> *With respect to Phonograph Records embodying Master Recordings made hereunder, together with other master recordings, the royalty rate payable to you shall be computed by multiplying the royalty rate other-wise applicable by a fraction, the numerator of which is the number of Sides contained thereon embodying Master Recordings made hereunder and the denominator of which is the total number of Sides contained on such Record; and*
>
> *With respect to Phonograph Records embodying Master Recordings made hereunder which embody your performances, together with the performances of another artist(s) to whom Company is obligated to pay royalties in respect of the sale of Phonograph Records derived form such Master Recordings, the royalty rate to be used in determining the royalties payable to you shall be computed by multiplying the royalty rate otherwise applicable thereto by a fraction, the numerator of which shall be one and the denominator of which shall be the total number of recording artists (including you) whose performances are embodied on such Master Recording.*

For instance, under the first provision, if Livin' Large releases a compilation album using two of Groove Therapy's masters, the company would not pay Groove Therapy 15% of the sales from the entire album. If the company paid Groove Therapy the full 15%, not only would Groove Therapy (and the other artists) be paid a percentage of sales on masters for which they had done no work, Livin' Large could be obligated to pay in excess of 100% of the net sales if the royalties were not pro-rated (that is, if there were 10 artists on the album and each artist received 15%, Livin' Large would be obligated to pay 150% in artist royalties). Therefore, if there were 12 tracks on the album, Groove Therapy would get 2/12 of its regular 15% royalty rate, or 2.5% of net sales from the album. The same would apply if Groove Therapy decided to team up with a separate solo artist to release a single. Livin' Large would reduce each artist's rate by 1/2, since there would be two royalty receiving artists on the track.

Although records may be counted as sold when shipped for some purposes, record companies should not pay royalties on units until the record company is actually paid.

> *No royalties shall be payable to you in respect of Phonograph Records sold by Company or its Licensees until payment for such Records has been received by Company, or for Phonograph Records sold as cut-outs after the listing of such Records has been deleted from the catalog of Company or the particular Licensee, or for scrap at a salvage or close-out price, or for less than fifty (50%) percent of Company's or its Licensee's regular wholesale price for such Records, or in respect of Phonograph Records distributed for promotional purposes or Phonograph Records sold or distributed to radio stations or for use on transportation carriers and facilities to promote or stimulate the sale of Phonograph Records, or in respect of Phonograph Records sold or distributed as "free" or "no-charge" or "bonus" Records (whether or not intended for resale); and*
>
> *Notwithstanding anything to the contrary contained hereinabove, in respect of the sale by Company to its dealers or distributors of Phonograph Records subject to a discount or merchandising plan, the number of Records deemed to have been sold shall be determined by reducing the number of Records shipped by the percentage of discount granted, and if a discount is granted in the form of "free" or "no-charge" Records such "free" or "no-charge" Records shall not be deemed included in the number of Records sold.*

The contract should also make it clear that royalties will not be paid on goods given away for promotional purposes or sold as scrap once deleted from the record company's catalog. Furthermore, where record companies and their distributors offer discounts in order to increase sales, the artist's royalties should be reduced.

As discussed above, the record company will not pay the artist any royalties until all advances are recouped.

> *No royalty shall be payable to you unless and until Company has recouped all Advances and all Recording Costs in connection with the Master Recordings produced hereunder from the royalties payable to you in respect of Net Sales of Phonograph Records embodying such Master Recordings, and after such recoupment, royalties shall be computed and*

paid to you only on those Records sold by Company or its Licensees after such recoupment.

The royalty payable to you hereunder includes all royalties due you, the individual producers and all other Persons in connection with the sale of Records or other exploitation of Masters made hereunder.

The record company should apply all artist royalties earned toward the repayment of advances, then pay remaining royalties directly to the artist. In addition, any producer or mixer royalties are deducted from the artist's royalties. The record company is not technically responsible for paying a non-company producer or mixer—that responsibility falls to the artist—but will generally do so as an accommodation to the artist. Therefore, if Groove Therapy offered a producer 3% to produce the album, then Groove Therapy would earn only 12% in artist royalties. As a side note, producers are not held responsible for the advances to the artist, although producers must generally wait until hard recording costs are recouped to receive their money. Therefore, even though Groove Therapy may not be paid any artist royalties due to the promotional costs assessed against them, the producer is entitled to royalties. After the hard recording costs are recouped, the record company will generally pay the producer his percentage, and that payment will be retroactive to the first album sold. Here's how it works: the record company will set aside the producer's 3% from the very first album, calculating recoupment of advances at a rate of 12% instead of 15%, but will not actually pay out the producer's money until all hard recording costs are recouped. At that time, the producer is paid the 3% that has been set aside, and the record company continues to pay the producer's 3% from that point on, recouping against the artist's remaining 12%. If the hard costs are never recouped, then the producer does not receive his royalties.

As discussed above, royalties may be calculated on either a wholesale or retail basis. Record companies will generally reserve the right to switch the basis for their calculation from one to the other.

Company may at some time change the method by which it computes royalties from a retail basis to some other basis (the "New Basis"), such as, without limitation, a wholesale basis. The New Basis will replace the then-current Royalty Base Price and the royalty rates will be adjusted to the appropriate royalty which, when applied to the New Basis, will yield the same dollar royalty amounts payable with respect to the Record concerned as was payable immediately prior to the change to the New Basis. If a Record was not theretofore sold in a particular configuration or at a particular price (e.g., a Budget Record), the adjusted royalty rate for any such configuration will be the adjusted royalty rate on top-line Albums multiplied by a fraction, the numerator of which is the royalty rate for sales in the configuration concerned prior to the New Basis and the denominator of which is the royalty rate for sales of top-line Albums prior to the New Basis. If there are other adjustments made by Company that would otherwise make the New Basis more favorable (a particular example of which might be the distribution of smaller quantities of free goods than theretofore distributed), then the benefits of such other adjustments will be taken into consideration in adjusting the royalty rate.

If the company switches its basis, the end-result should be the same dollar amount as the artist receives under the old basis. If there have been no sales under the old basis from which to establish a dollar amount, then the clause provides a formula for pro-rating the royalty rate.

Biz Note: Frequently, in order to combat the unrecouped album issue, generous record companies enter "partnership" deals with their artists, which result in a royalty of 50% to the artist. Although there is nothing at all wrong with being generous, be *very* careful when making this kind of deal. Even when it's net profit you're splitting, you have to take operating expenses out of your half. The artist doesn't. Therefore, the artist takes home money free and clear, and the label spends its entire half on overhead and has nothing left (and frequently goes in the hole).

J. Accountings

Even when the artist is not receiving royalties, the record company should provide an accounting of what royalties the artist is earning and where the money is going. Accounting provisions will outline how often the artist gets a statement, what rights the artist has to review the record company's books and contest the statements, and how monies received in foreign currency will be accounted for.

Company shall compute royalties payable to you hereunder as of June 30th and December 31st for each preceding six (6) month period during which Records as to which royalties are payable hereunder are sold, and, prior to each succeeding September 30 and March 31st, respectively, shall render a statement and pay the net amount of such royalties, if any, less any unrecouped Advances and any other permissible offsets, including, without limitation, such amounts, if any, that Company may be required to withhold pursuant to the applicable state tax laws, the U.S. Tax Regulations, or any other applicable statute, regulation, treaty, or law. Company will liquidate any reserves within two (2) full accounting periods after the period in which such reserves were initially established. No royalty statements will be required for periods during which no additional royalties accrue. Company may deduct from any royalty or other payment due to you under this Agreement, any amount you may owe Company under this Agreement and/or any other agreement between you and Company or its affiliates, including products purchased under this Agreement. If Company makes any overpayment to you (e.g., by reason of an accounting error or by paying royalties on Records returned later), you will reimburse Company to the extent Company does not deduct such sums from monies due you hereunder.

Many record companies account to artists every six months. Although the record company will not provide an accounting when no royalties are earned, it should provide a statement when royalties are accrued and then paid toward an outstanding advance. This clause provides that the record company will apply earned royalties toward outstanding amounts owed, including advances and any over payments. It also shows that reserves are liquidated after one year. The liquidation period varies from company to company, but one year is a good average.

Foreign sales raise additional issues, such as different retail prices, rates of exchange and time required for payment. Therefore, the record company will usually include a clause similar to this one.

Royalties for Records sold for distribution outside of the United States of America (the "foreign sales") shall be computed in the national currency in which Company is paid by its Licensees and shall be paid to you at the same rate of exchange at which Company is paid. For accounting purposes, foreign sales shall be deemed to occur in the same semi-annual accounting periods in which Company's Licensees account to Company therefor. If Company is unable, for reasons beyond its control, to receive payment for such sales in United States Dollars in the United States of America, royalties therefor shall not be credited to your account during the continuance of such inability; if any accounting rendered to you hereunder during the continuance of such inability requires the payment of royalties to you, Company will, at your request and if Company is able to do so, deposit such royalties to your credit in such foreign currency in a foreign depository, at your expense.

Most record companies license foreign sales to other companies, which account to the record company in a similar manner as record companies account to artists. The record company is unable to account to the artist until its licensees render their accountings. Furthermore, the record company will want to ensure that the artist is paid at the same exchange rate as the company and that, if the company cannot obtain payment in the currency of the contract, it will not be forced to render accountings or payments until the situation is remedied. In fact, as noted in this provision, if the record company must, for whatever reason, pay artist royalties and cannot convert the currency, it may deposit the royalties in a foreign account in the foreign currency and at the artist's expense.

Although the time periods may vary from contract to contract, most recording artist agreements will contain provisions that limit the time after which an artist receives a statement that the artist may contest the validity of the statement.

At any time within two (2) years after any royalty statement is rendered to you hereunder, you shall have the right to give Company written notice of your intention to examine Company's books and records with respect to such statement. Such examination shall be commenced within six (6) months after the date of such notice, at your sole cost and expense, by any certified public accountant or attorney designated by you, provided he or she is not then engaged in an outstanding examination of Company's books and records on behalf of a person other than you. Such examination shall be made during Company's usual business hours at the place where Company maintains the books and records which relate to you and which are necessary to verify the accuracy of the statement or statements specified in your notice to Company and your examination shall be limited to the foregoing. Your right to inspect Company's books and records shall be only as set forth in this paragraph and Company shall have no obligation to produce such books and records more than once with respect to each statement rendered to you.

Unless notice is given to Company as provided in herein, each royalty statement rendered to you shall be final, conclusive and binding on you and shall constitute an account stated. You shall be foreclosed from maintaining any action, claim or proceeding against Company in any forum or tribunal with respect to any statement or accounting rendered hereunder unless such action, claim or proceeding is commenced against Company within one (1) year after the completion of examination set forth hereinabove.

For instance under these two provisions, if an artist doesn't protest the statement by giving the company notice within two years after it is rendered, then follow up with an audit by an accountant or attorney within six months of the notice, the artist waives the right to protest the statement at all. In fact, even if the artist protests within the two year time frame and audits within six months after the notice, the artist has one year to resolve the discrepancies with the company or file a legal action. If the artist doesn't file a lawsuit within a year after the audit, any unresolved discrepancies are waived.

The provisions also limit how the statement can be contested. The audit cannot be performed by the artist. It must be performed by a certified accountant or attorney. The records are limited to those that directly pertain to the artist. Furthermore, once the audit is complete, the same records cannot be audited a second time.

Biz Note: If there's one thing that will get a label in trouble, its failure to render accountings to artists. Many record labels get caught up in the recording and releasing of new projects and don't even think about taking care of business for the old ones. Nothing will make an artist more suspicious, and more likely to start sending breach of contract letters, than a failure to account. It doesn't matter if the album has only sold 1,000 copies and is in the hole by $30,000. If there have been any sales, make a timely accounting.

K. Publishing Matters

Publishing rights can be a significant source of income. As such, artists who are also songwriters have much more to offer and much more to protect. From the record company's perspective, the extra income stream can be an incentive for signing an artist in whom the company will have to invest significant income that it may not recover. However, many artists that understand the significance of publishing are reluctant to sign it away without some incentive. This key element of income should be well understood before entering into negotiations with your artist.

So what is music publishing, then? A complete discussion of music publishing could fill a book in and of itself. However, perhaps a simple illustration will help. The members of our group Groove Therapy, Fred, Joe and Bob, write all of their own materials. Therefore, you can really think of them as two distinct groups: Fred, Joe and Bob, the songwriters and Groove Therapy, the recording artist. As the group Groove Therapy, the three make artist royalties from recording songs onto the album that Livin' Large distributes. They would make this money even if they did not write their own material. However, keep in mind that they only make this money after all of their recording costs and other advances are recouped.

Fred, Joe and Bob, as individuals, make money as composers of musical compositions. Once a songwriter writes a song, someone must be responsible for promoting the song so that an artist will want to record it on an album (when an artist records another songwriter's composition, it is called a "cover"). Therefore, Fred, Joe and Bob would assign half of the income in each song they write to a publisher owned by them, Sky's the Limit Music. Sky's the Limit then "shops" the songs to find artists to cover them. In Fred, Joe and Bob's case, that wouldn't seem to be too difficult—they have a band with a recording contract, right? However, assume that the guys have written a song that is guaranteed to be a hit country song, but Livin' Large only releases rock music. Sky's the Limit shops around until it finds a country band, Honkey Tonk Special, to record the song on its upcoming album. You can see that the band Groove Therapy makes no money because it doesn't have anything to do here. Honkey Tonk Special, however, would make the artist royalties and would have to pay the songwriter and publisher for the right to record the song (called mechanical royalties). Therefore, Sky's the Limit takes half of the income as the publishers, and Fred, Joe and Bob split the remaining income as the songwriters.

Because composers are responsible only for writing the songs, the recording costs of any albums that the songs may end up on are not their problem. Consider the above example—why should Fred, Joe and Bob be responsible for recording costs on Honkey Tonk Special's album, when they are making no artist royalties and didn't record on the album? Therefore, the mechanical royalties are not recouped against. Furthermore, songwriting royalties extend beyond the recording of albums—live performances on stage, airplay on a radio, even songs played over the loud speakers in a restaurant will earn money, called performance royalties.

Assignment of publishing rights

Returning to the recording artist agreement, then, why are we even talking about publishing when the artist and the songwriter/publisher are two separate entities? Because some record companies merge the artist and the songwriter in an attempt to capitalize off of this extra income stream. This is fairly common for independent record companies. Album sales for small labels may not be sufficient incentive to risk large amounts of money on new artists, so publishing income adds extra revenue to the package. In any event, some labels will attempt to take a partial or full assignment of publishing. From the record company's standpoint, this provides added security and additional income.

This is an example of a provision that assigns a portion of publishing to a record company's designated publisher:

> *You hereby irrevocably and absolutely assign, convey and set over to Company and/or Company's publishing designee a fifty (50%) right, title and interest (including the worldwide copyright and all extensions and renewals of such copyrights) in and to each and every Controlled Composition that is recorded hereunder. You agree to execute and deliver to Company (or Company's affiliated music publishing company or to any other publishing company designated by Company), a separate Songwriter's Agreement in respect to each Controlled Composition subject to the provisions of this paragraph, in the form of Exhibit "A" attached hereto and made a part hereof by this reference. All the terms and conditions of said Songwriter's Agreement shall govern the respective rights and obligations of the parties with respect to such Controlled Compositions. If you shall fail to promptly execute such Songwriter's Agreement, you hereby irrevocably grant to Company a power of attorney to execute said agreement in your name.*

You should note that the provision assigns "50% right, title and interest in and to each and every controlled composition." This can be a source of much confusion. The publishing is half of the interest in a composition, so it would appear that this clause assigns all of the publishing. Actually, it only assigns half of the publishing, or 25% of the total interest in the song. So why does it say "50% right, title and interest"? When a songwriter assigns publishing, he or she assigns all of the copyright and retains only the right to collect the songwriting income. Therefore, since half of the copyright is assigned, then only half of the publishing is assigned. The remaining half of the copyright would go to the songwriter's personal publisher, and the songwriter retains all songwriting income, which is half of the song's total income.

Returning to our example, if this clause appeared in Groove Therapy's contract, then Fred, Joe and Bob would assign half of the copyright in all of their compositions (even the ones that Groove Therapy does not record) to Livin' Large's publisher and half to Sky's the Limit. Livin' Large would likely be responsible for all of the administrative tasks in connection with the song, including issuing licenses and collecting money. If Livin' Large's publisher received $100 in mechanical royalties, it would divide that amount in half. $50 would be divided between Fred, Joe and Bob as the songwriters, and $50 would be divided between Livin' Large and Sky's the Limit as the publishers.

Controlled Compositions

If a record company does not accept assignment of any publishing, there are still ways that the company can make money from publishing. Record companies may include in the agreement a provision that would limit the amount of money paid on a so-called "controlled composition." A controlled composition is a song written or owned by an individual who is a member of the artist. In our example, a controlled composition would be any song written by Fred, Joe or Bob, or a song written by someone else, if that person assigned any publishing to Sky's the Limit. By law, a song that has been published can be recorded by anyone, as long as the rate prescribed in the law is paid to the songwriter and publisher.

However, it is always possible to negotiate a lower rate, if the publisher wishes to agree to that rate (and when faced with a reduced income from the recording or none at all if the song is excluded from the recording, many publishers will). This is where the recording artist agreement takes over. A recording artist agreement may limit the amount of mechanical royalties paid on controlled compositions to a percentage of the going rate. So, if Groove Therapy's recording contract contains a limitation such as this, they might only get 75% of the going rate for the mechanical royalties.

Following is an example of a clause that addresses controlled compositions. First, the record company takes a permanent license to record any songs written or owned by its artist:

a.   *You hereby grant Company, its distributors and its licensees, an irrevocable license under copyright to reproduce each Controlled Composition on records and to distribute them throughout the Territory.*

Then the record company ensures that, if the artist sells or gives away the composition's ownership to someone else, the record company's rights remain intact:

b.   *Any assignment made of the ownership of copyrights, or of the rights to license or administer the use of any Controlled Compositions, shall be subject to the terms and provisions hereof.*

The agreement will also make sure that any songs used that are not owned by the artist will be properly licensed, under reasonable terms, before appearing on the album:

c.   *If any Album made under this Agreement contains compositions that are not Controlled Compositions, you will obtain licenses covering those compositions on terms no less favorable to Company than those contained in the then-current standard mechanical license issued by The Harry Fox Agency, Inc. You will also cause to be issued to Company licenses to reproduce each non-Controlled Composition on records distributed in the rest of the universe on terms as favorable as those generally prevailing in the country concerned.*

Then, as discussed above, the record company will take its license to record the artist's songs (and, for that matter, songs not owned by the artist) at a percentage of the going rate, here 75%:

d.   *You hereby agree to grant Company a mechanical license to reproduce each Controlled Composition for a royalty equal to seventy five percent (75%) of the minimum applicable statutory rate in effect in the United States or other applicable country on the date of the first commercial release of the record. If the copyright law of any given country does not provide for a minimum compulsory rate, but the major record companies and major music publishers in such country have agreed to a mechanical license rate (the "Agreed Rate"), you agree to grant Company a mechanical license to reproduce each Controlled Composition for a royalty equal to seventy five percent (75%) of the Agreed Rate in effect on the date of the first commercial release of the record. With respect to non-Controlled Compositions you shall use your best efforts to assist Company in obtaining similar terms from the copyright owner.*

You might wonder what happens if the artist approaches another songwriter to cover a song and is unable to procure the 75% rate. The record company expects the artist to cover the difference between the 75% and the rate the artist is actually able to procure:

> *You agree to indemnify and hold Company harmless from the payment of Mechanical Royalties in excess of the applicable herein. If Company pays any such excess, such payments will be a direct debt from you to Company, which, in addition to any other remedies available, Company may recover such excess from royalties or any other payments hereunder.*

So if Fred absolutely insists that the band *must* record a song called "Diva in Las Vegas" recorded by the Plastic Rainbows five years ago, the record company will allow them to cover that song. However, if the publisher that owns "Diva in Las Vegas" wants 100% of the going rate, Groove Therapy will have to pay the 25% difference if it wants to record the song.

Another way that recording artist agreements reduce the record company's costs to publishers is to put a cap on the number of songs for which they will pay mechanical royalties:

> e. *Subject to subparagraph 22(f), and notwithstanding anything else to the contrary contained herein, the maximum combined rate for all Compositions on each Album shall not exceed ten (10) times seventy five percent (75%) of such minimum applicable statutory or Agreed Rate ("Mechanical Royalty Cap"). To the extent that Company is required to pay mechanical royalties in excess of such Mechanical Royalty Cap, Company may deduct such excess from any and all monies otherwise payable to Artist hereunder.*

To illustrate, let's say that on Groove Therapy's first album, there were a total of 13 songs. However, their contract noted that the record company would only pay mechanical royalties for a total of 10 songs (i.e. "shall not exceed ten (10) times" the rate). Therefore, Groove Therapy recorded three songs for which the songwriters and publishers received no mechanical royalties at all.

Putting these provisions together, you can see how it is possible for a record company to drastically reduce the amount of money it pays for publishing royalties. In our above example, if Fred, Joe and Bob retained all publishing, were paid the full rate for controlled compositions, and were paid for each song on the album, their publishing and songwriting income would look like this:

250,000 albums x 13 songs x $0.085 per song (current as of 1/1/2005) = $276,250 due Fred, Joe, Bob and Sky's the Limit

However, if the record company paid only 75% of the going rate, and only paid for 10 of 13 songs, the songwriting income would look something like this:

250,000 albums x 10 songs x $0.06375 per song (i.e. $0.085 x 75%) = $159,375

AND if the record company took all of their publishing, the record company would retain half of that sum because publishing income is half of the mechanical royalties:

$159,375 ÷ 2 = $79,687.5 due Fred, Joe and Bob

This example illustrates two things: 1) if Livin' Large's contract contains all of these provisions, it saved $196,562.50; and 2) why publishing is so important—after 250,000 albums, Groove Therapy still owes the record company a substantial amount of money, but the songwriters have generated $276,250 of income that is not recouped against.

Biz Note: Some record companies will attempt to "cross collateralize" against artists who write their own music by recouping artist expenses against songwriter income and vice versa. This practice is generally frowned upon, but can be considered in unusual circumstances.

L. Warranties

As you will see in many of the agreements contained in this book, before a company is willing to spend any money on the artist, the artist has to make certain guarantees and promises. If the guarantees turn out to be incorrect, the record company will have a provision to point to in order to remedy whatever problem the faulty guarantee causes.

Common guarantees include: a guarantee that the artist is old enough to legally sign a contract and is not under a contract with anyone else that would interfere with the recording agreement:

You are under no disability, restriction or prohibition, whether contractual or otherwise, with respect to your right to enter into this

Agreement and your right to grant the rights granted to Company hereunder, to perform each and every term and provision hereof, and to record each and every Composition hereunder...;

a guarantee that the record company is not going to need to pay anyone other than the artist for any of the rights that it is trying to acquire:

Company shall not be required to make any payments of any nature for, or in connection with, the acquisition, exercise or exploitation of rights by Company pursuant to this Agreement, except as specifically provided in this Agreement...;

a guarantee that if any union has jurisdiction, the artist has joined and is complying with the union rules:

You are or will become and will remain to the extent necessary to enable the performance of this Agreement, a member in good standing of all labor unions or guilds, membership in which may be lawfully required for the performance of your services hereunder...;

a guarantee that the compositions or any other material supplied by the artist belong to artist and are not going to infringe on anyone else's rights:

Neither the "Materials" nor any use of the Materials by Company will violate any law or infringe upon any rights of any Person. "Materials" as used in this subparagraph means any musical, artistic and literary materials, ideas and other intellectual properties, furnished by you and contained in or used in connection with any Recordings made hereunder or the packaging, sale, distribution, advertising, publicizing or other exploitation thereof...;

and a guarantee that the artist has not recorded any masters that the record company is unaware of:

There are now in existence no prior recorded performances by you unreleased within the United States of America and elsewhere in the world....

In addition to the guarantees, the artist also has to make promises, in addition to the obvious promises to record the album, to appear for interviews and conduct live performances. The artist also will have to promise not to obligate him or herself to anything that might interfere with his or her ability to deliver what the recording contract is asking for:

> *During the Term of this Agreement, you will not enter into any agreement which would interfere with the full and prompt performance of your obligations hereunder, and you will not perform or render any services for the purpose of making Phonograph Records or Master Recordings for any person other than Company.*

In order to restrict direct competition against the record company for the masters that it will pay for during the term, the artist will also have to promise not to re-record any of the songs recorded during the agreement (whether or not the artist wrote the song) for a certain period of time after the agreement expires.

> *After the expiration of the Term of this Agreement, for any reason whatsoever, you will not perform any Composition which shall have been recorded hereunder for any person other than Company for the purpose of making Phonograph Records or Master Recordings prior to the date five (5) years subsequent to the expiration date of the Term of the Agreement.*

Although the contract will state separately that the artist's services are exclusive, the artist must also promise not to record for any other record company during the term of the agreement:

> *You will not at any time record, manufacture, distribute or sell, or authorize or knowingly permit your performances to be recorded by any party for any purpose without an express written agreement prohibiting the use of such Recording on Phonograph Records in violation of the foregoing restrictions.*

The artist will promise to assist in policing the recordings. If the artist becomes aware that someone is distributing the masters without authorization, he or she will have to report this to the record company:

> *In the event that you shall become aware of any unauthorized recording, manufacture, distribution or sale by any third party contrary to the foregoing re-recording restrictions, you shall notify Company*

thereof and shall cooperate with Company in the event that Company commences any action or proceeding against such third party.

M. Indemnity

Nearly every contract that a recording artist or songwriter signs will contain an indemnity provision, so you will see this type of language several times throughout the book. An indemnity is a promise to pay if there is a legal claim against the record company based on any of the artist's work. Although there are several areas where law suits crop up, the most common example is where a recording artist writes and records a song, then someone else claims rights in the song. Based on the division of responsibility between artists and songwriters we have discussed in this chapter, you may wonder why someone would sue an artist for a songwriter issue. Using a previous example, should Honkey Tonk Special be sued if it did not know that Floyd was a contributing author to Fred, Joe and Bob's song? Although the answer is technically no, the distinction can be difficult to grasp, especially if the artist and the songwriter are one and the same. Furthermore, the copyright issues are fairly complex and many, many people do not understand how they work. Therefore, the artist may get sued anyway, and, accordingly, so does their record company. When this happens, the artist must repay the record company for any losses it may suffer resulting from such a claim:

You will at all times indemnify and hold harmless Company and any Licensee of Company from and against any and all claims, damages, liabilities, costs and expenses, including legal expenses and reasonable counsel fees, arising out of any alleged breach or actual breach by you of any warranty, representation or agreement made by you herein. You will reimburse Company and/or its Licensees on demand for any payment made at any time after the date hereof in respect of any liability or claim in respect of which Company or its Licensees are entitled to be indemnified. Upon the making or filing of any such claim, action or demand, Company shall be entitled to withhold from any amounts payable under this Agreement such amounts as are reasonably related to the potential liability at issue. You shall be notified of any such claim, action or demand and shall have the right, at your own expense, to participate in the defense thereof with counsel of your own choosing; provided, however, that Company's decision in connection with the defense of any such claim, action or demand shall be final.

It is important to note that losses include attorney's fees, even if the lawsuit has no merit and the case is won. Copyright infringement suits can run attorneys fees and costs well into the six figure range, regardless of the verdict. Therefore, the artist should understand that, even though he or she believes that the claim is false and there is nothing to be concerned about, the mere fact that a claim exists could be costly. By now, it should come as no surprise that the record company can deduct its losses from the artist's royalties.

N. Definitions

Recording agreements can contain pages and pages (and pages) of defined terms, most of which do not need discussion. However, there are a couple of terms that bear mentioning, because they are key to understanding how royalties are calculated and may not be mentioned anywhere else in the agreement.

> *Container Charge—with respect to cassette tapes, compact discs, videos, DVDs, CD ROMs and CD Singles, and other configurations, twenty-five percent (25%) of the applicable Wholesale Selling Price of such Phonograph Records.*

The container charge is exactly that—it is a charge that represents the packaging that the compact disc or cassette comes in. The artist is paid a royalty for its performance of the music, not for the jewel case that the music comes in, nor for the paper included with the album. Therefore, the record company should deduct a predetermined percentage from the selling price of the album in order to account for that. The percentages range from twenty five percent on the low end to forty percent on the high end.

> *Royalty Base Price—the applicable suggested Wholesale/Retail Selling Price of Phonograph Records less all taxes, distribution expenses and applicable Container Charge.*

This provision is an example of deductions from royalties that may otherwise be missed. When you look at the provision labeled "Royalties," you may not see anything except for a provision similar to that contained in section H, above:

> *Fifteen Percent (15%) of the Royalty Base Price in connection with the Sale Through Normal Retail Channels in the United States of America of Phonograph Records in disc, tape, or other forms.*

However, look at how the provision is phrased—not fifteen percent of the selling price, but fifteen percent of the "Royalty Base Price." Because the term is capitalized, you must apply the definition of "Royalty Base Price" so that you can see exactly what the percentage is applied to.

An example may help. According to their contract with Livin' Large, Groove Therapy is to receive a fifteen percent royalty, based on the Royalty Base Price, as defined in the definitions section. Depending upon how the record company calculates royalties, the starting point would be either the retail selling price or the wholesale selling price. Let's assume that the record company pays royalties on retail price, $15.95. The calculation would look something like this:

Retail Price - 25% Container Charge - 20% Distribution Charge - 23% Reserves = Royalty Base Price

$15.95 - $3.99 - $3.19 - $3.67 = $5.10

Therefore, the artist's royalty would be 15% of $5.10, or $0.77 per unit sold. Naturally, each record company's accountings and reductions are a little different, and some of these costs may be adjusted or eliminated for artists with more bargaining power. However, this illustrates that a "15%" royalty is not exactly as it appears, and you must look at how each term is defined to understand what deductions may apply.

O. Suspension and Termination

Naturally, the record company should expect the artist to live up to his or her promises during the term of the contract.

> a. *If at any time you fail, except solely for Company's refusal without cause to allow you to perform, to fulfill your recording commitment within the times set forth herein, then, without limiting Company's rights, Company shall have the option, exercisable at any time by notice to you, to (i) terminate this Agreement without any further obligation to you as to unrecorded Master Recordings, or (ii) to suspend Company's obligations to you hereunder during the period of default, and/or (iii) to extend the expiration date of the current period of the Term for the period of the default plus such additional time as is necessary so that Company shall have no less than one hundred twenty (120) days after completion of your recording*

commitment within which to exercise its option, if any, for the next following contract year. If Company terminates this Agreement, Company may require you to repay the amount not then recouped of any Advance previously paid by Company that is not specifically attributable to an album that has been delivered hereunder.

b.   *If Artist becomes physically unable to perform recording and/or personal appearances and/or if Artist ceases to pursue a career as an entertainer, Company will have the right to terminate the term of this agreement by notice to you at any time during the period in which such contingency continues and thereby be relieved of any liability for the executory provisions of this agreement.*

If the artist fails to perform (or becomes unable to perform), the record company will want to either terminate the contract (and demand repayment of advances) or suspend the running of the term until the artist remedies any failure that might have occurred. This simply means that the contract term will be extended by the amount of time that passes while the artist is in breach of the contract, plus the additional time that it will take for the record company to decide whether another album will be feasible.

The record company also has to live up to its promises. However, if the record company chooses not to honor the contract, the options available to the artist are a little different.

b.   *If, in respect of any contract year of the Term of this Agreement, Company fails, without cause, to allow you to fulfill your Minimum Recording Commitment within nine (9) months following the commencement of any Contract Period and if, within thirty (30) days after the expiration of such nine (9) month period you shall notify Company of your desire to fulfill such Minimum Recording Commitment, then Company shall permit you to fulfill said Minimum Recording Commitment by notice to you to such effect within sixty (60) days of Company's receipt of your notice. Should Company fail to give such notice, you shall have the option within thirty (30) days after the expiration of said sixty (60) day period to give Company notice that you wish to terminate the Term of this Agreement; on receipt by Company of such notice, the Term of this Agreement shall terminate and all parties will be deemed to have fulfilled all of the obligations hereunder, except those obligations which survive the end of the Term (e.g., warranties, re-recording restrictions and obligations to pay royalties). In the event you fail to give Company either notice within the period specified therefor, Company shall be under no obligation to you for failing to permit you to fulfill such Minimum Recording Commitment or otherwise.*

If the record company executes the contract, or exercises an option, then fails to allow the artist to proceed with recording the album, the artist may usually terminate the contract. However, before the termination occurs, the artist must follow the instructions contained in the contract. According to this provision, the record company must have nine months to allow the artist to commence with recording. If, after nine months has passed, the record company has not allowed the recording to take place, the artist has only thirty days to send the record company an official notice (instructions for official notices are contained elsewhere in the contract) that the artist wants to proceed with the recording. If the artist does not send the notice exactly as the contract provides for notices to be sent and within the thirty-day period, then the artist cannot take any further action.

Once the record company gets the artist's letter, the record company has sixty days to allow recording to commence. If the artist does not receive a letter from the record company, stating that the record company will allow the recording to take place, within sixty days after the record company first receives the artist's notice, then the artist must send another letter. This letter, which also must be sent within thirty days, must state that the artist wishes to terminate the contract.

Sound complicated? In essence, the record company can terminate the contract as soon as the artist breaches the contract. The artist, however, must give the record company a lot of notice and a lot of time to cure its default. If the artist does not act exactly as the contract describes, then the artist waives his or her right to do anything at all. This recognizes the reality that record companies are dealing with multiple contracts, and the artist is dealing only with one. Therefore, the record company should provide itself with plenty of room to realize that a breach has occurred and fix the problem before the artist can abandon the contract.

Another contingency that is usually addressed is *force majeure*. If an act of God, government or other circumstances beyond the company's control hinders the record company's performance, then the record company will want to prevent termination of the contract.

c.   *If, because of an act of God, inevitable accident, fire, lockout, strike or other labor dispute, riot or civil commotion, act of public enemy, enactment, rule, order or act of any government or governmental instrumentality (whether federal, state, local or foreign), failure of technical facilities, failure or delay of transportation facilities, illness or incapacity of any performer or producer, or other cause of a similar or different nature not reasonably within Company's control, Company is materially hampered in the recording, manufacture, distribution or sale of Records, or Company's normal business operations become commercially impractical, then, without limiting Company's rights, Company shall have the option by giving you notice to suspend the Term of this Agreement for the duration of any such contingency plus such additional time as is necessary so that Company shall have no less than thirty (30) days after the cessation of such contingency in which to exercise its option, if any, for the next following option period. Any such extension of the then current Contract Year due to any cause set forth in this Paragraph 14(c) which involves only Company shall be limited to a period of six (6) months.*

If the record company is unable to perform because of a disaster, the agreement is suspended until the company can regain its ability to perform. Although some recording agreements do not place any limitations on any such suspension, this agreement limits suspensions to six months.

Record companies, especially independent labels, frequently have trouble getting properly signed documents from busy artists. Therefore, record companies should include a provision giving them the right to suspend royalties until all documents have been received:

d.   *You agree that Company may suspend payment of any amounts due you under this Agreement, including without limitation artist royalties, songwriter royalties and publisher royalties, if you breach any warranty or representation made herein or if you fail to deliver any documents or any information requested by Company that is necessary to secure all rights for Company in each Album. You agree that such suspension may continue until you have complied with Company's requests and/or cured any breach hereunder.*

Biz note: Always, always, *always* insist on signed documents. Many record labels continue to pay royalties to artists that neglect to return documents because they want to stay on good terms with the artist. If the artist realizes any manner of success and you don't have your documents signed, you *will* be over a barrel. If you have already given the artist what they want (their advance, album is released, royalty checks paid, etc.), then they have no reason to return the signed documents to you. Hold the money and the release until the contracts are signed.

P. Group Provisions

Many times an artist, such as our example "Groove Therapy," will consist of more than one member. In that case, the record company will want to ensure that all band members are bound by the agreement.

If you are comprised of more than one (1) individual:

a.   *Your obligations under the terms of this Agreement are joint and several and all references to you shall include all members comprising you jointly and each member comprising you individually, unless otherwise specifically provided herein.*

b.   *Any breach of this Agreement by any of the persons comprising you shall be deemed to be a breach by all of the persons comprising you.*

Furthermore, when there is more than one person serving as the artist, there will be a band name, rather than just an individual's name. The entire group must guarantee that the name they are using belongs to them.

c.   *You represent and warrant that you are the sole owner of any and every group name now used or hereafter adopted by you insofar as rights of ownership can be acquired in a group name; that no other person or persons have the right to use said group name or to authorize or license its use in connection with Records; that you have the full right and authority to grant to Company all of the rights to use said group name as is contemplated in this Agreement.*

Most bands firmly believe that the name they have chosen is absolutely original. However, there have been many situations where a band was prepared to sign with a record label only to discover that another band had registered a federal trademark using that very name. Few things will bring on a lawsuit faster than a successful album, and if there is one rule for entertainment industry lawsuits, it is that *everybody* gets sued—individual band members, the record company, the distributor, etc. This is precisely why the record company should not sign a band without this promise. Check the band's name to make sure it isn't taken, then follow up with a trademark registration to protect the name from others.

Another frequent occurrence when dealing with multiple member artists is band break ups. For many different reasons, including differences of opinion, illness or death of a member, and changes in life goals, band members leave and are replaced by new band members. The agreement will make provision for this possibility.

> d.   *If any member comprising you shall cease to perform as a member of the group, the following provisions shall apply:*
>
>> i.   *You shall promptly notify Company thereof and such leaving member shall be replaced by a new member, and such new member shall be subject to Company's approval. Such approved new member shall thereafter be deemed substituted as a party to this Agreement in the place of such leaving member and shall automatically be bound by all the terms and conditions of this Agreement. Upon Company's request, you will cause any such new member to execute and deliver to Company such documents as Company, in its judgment, may deem necessary or advisable to effectuate the foregoing sentence. Thereafter, the leaving member shall no longer be required to render his recording services hereunder as a member of the group, but you (and such leaving member individually) shall continue to be bound by the other provisions of this Agreement, including, without limitation, subparagraph (d)(iv) below;*
>>
>> ii.   *Notwithstanding anything to the contrary contained herein, Company shall have the right to terminate the Term of this Agreement by written notice given to you at any time prior to the expiration of ninety (90) days after Company's receipt of your said notice to Company. In the event of such termination, all of the members comprising you shall be deemed leaving members as of the date of such termination notice, and subparagraph (d)(iv) below shall be applicable to you;*
>>
>> iii.   *Each leaving member hereby relinquishes all of his rights in the group name to the remaining members of the group; and*
>>
>> iv.   *Company shall have, and you hereby grant to Company, an option to engage the exclusive services of such leaving member*

as a recording artist ("Leaving Member Option"). Such Leaving Member Option may be exercised by Company by notice at any time prior to the expiration of ninety (90) days after the date of (A) Company's receipt of your notice provided for in subparagraph (d)(i) above, or (B) Company's termination notice pursuant to subparagraph (d)(ii) above, as the case may be. If Company exercises such Leaving Member Option, the leaving member concerned shall be deemed to be bound by a new exclusive recording artist agreement (the "New Agreement") that contains the same terms and conditions as are contained herein, except that (i) the Commencement date of the New Agreement shall be the date Company exercises its Leaving Member Option, (ii) the Minimum Recording Commitment shall not exceed one (1) Album per Contract Year, and (iii) and the basic royalty rate shall be the basic royalty rate payable pursuant to this Agreement and (iv) no Advances otherwise payable to you shall be payable to the leaving member in the New Agreement.

The record company should expect some say-so in choosing any necessary replacement band members. Therefore, although the artist will generally select the replacement, the replacement is not effective until the record company agrees. Generally, the record company should not force a member on an unwilling band, simply because personality conflicts do not make for good quality records. However, the record company does not want the band selecting a person with marginal talent just because he or she is a friend. Most importantly, the record company will be concerned with the new member's willingness to abide by the terms of the contract.

It is important to note that the leaving member is not released from the contract, even if a new member takes his or her place. Although the leaving member will no longer be required to record with the group once he or she is replaced, the leaving member is still the record company's exclusive property. It should also be noted that the right to use the group's name stays with the remaining members. If there are no remaining members, *nobody* has the right to use the name. Frequently, a member will leave with the desire to release a solo album. The record company will not want the band member to be able to take his or her services to a competing record company simply because he or she is no longer a member of the group, especially if the leaving member was the key player in the group. Therefore, the record company will reserve a "leaving member option." The leaving member option will allow the record company the exclusive right to sign the leaving member to a record deal, as long as the agreement is similar to the agreement signed with the original band (including the termination date for the contract). When the key member leaves the group, the record company will also reserve the right to terminate the contract as to the remaining members, if the record company feels that the remaining members are no longer marketable as an artist, even with the addition of a replacement band member.

For instance, if Fred, Joe and Bob have a falling out and Fred, who is the group's lead singer and main songwriter, leaves the band, Livin' Large will exercise its leaving member option and sign Fred to a solo deal, thus preventing Fred from defecting to another record label. Livin' Large must then decide whether Joe and Bob will continue to be a viable group without Fred. Livin' Large could either continue its contract with Groove Therapy or decide that Groove Therapy is no longer a marketable artist without Fred. If Livin' Large terminates its contract with Groove Therapy, it could then pick up either Joe or Bob as solo artists.

Q. Merchandising

Many independent labels will want rights in the artist's merchandising (t-shirts, ball caps, keychains, posters and the like), either because the label is looking for additional income streams or because the artist has neither the money nor the know how to exploit the rights.

> *You hereby grant to Company and its Licensees the exclusive right, throughout the World, to use and authorize the use of your name, portraits, pictures, likenesses and biographical material, either alone or in conjunction with other elements, in connection with the sale, lease, licensing or other disposition of merchandising rights. For the rights granted by you to Company in this paragraph, Company shall pay to you a royalty of twenty-five (25%) percent of Company's net royalty receipts derived from the exploitation of such rights, after deducting all costs and third party payments relating thereto; and such royalty shall be accounted to you in the manner otherwise provided herein.*

Biz note: As a practical matter, most record companies stay out of the merchandising business. Record companies generally do not have the time or the staff to follow the band on tour and set up a merchandise table. However, where the artist simply cannot afford to capitalize on its own merchandising, the record company may provide funding and allow the artist to take the funds and use them to purchase and sell merchandise. As a general rule, whether the issue is merchandise or purchase of artist's product for sale on the road, the record company is best protected by producing the products, then having the artist pay for the product up front, as it is needed. Logistically, providing an artist with product then expecting the artist to sell it, account for it, and pay the record company its percentage after it is sold is *not* a good arrangement.

R. Videos

An integral part of any significant release is the music video that accompanies it. The record company will want the right to release a video, without being obligated to release one if they do not wish to. As with everything else, if the company elects to create a video, the company will own the product.

a. *Company, in its sole discretion, shall have the right, but not the obligation, to require you to perform at such times and places as Company designates for the production of Videos, subject to your reasonable availability. Company shall be the exclusive owner throughout the world and in perpetuity of the Videos, if any, and all rights therein, including all copyrights and renewal of copyrights, and shall have all of the rights with respect thereto which are set forth in herein, including without limitation the right (but not the obligation) to use and exploit Videos in any and all forms.*

b. *The producer, director, and concept or script for each video will be approved by both you and Company. Company will engage the producer, director and other production personnel for each video and will pay the production costs of each video in an amount not in excess of a budget to be established in advance by you and Company (the "Production Budget"). You will pay any and all production costs for each Video in excess of the Production Budget where such excess is caused by the acts or omissions of you or Artist, provided that if such excess is not caused by the acts or omissions of you or Artist, such excess will be an expense in connection with such video, recoupable in the same manner as costs incurred in connection with the Production Budget Notwithstanding the foregoing, if such excess is solely due to the wrongdoing of Company, you will not be required to pay such excess, but such excess will be an expense in connection with such video, recoupable in the same manner as costs incurred in connection with the Production*

Budget. In the event that Company pays any production costs that are your responsibility pursuant to the foregoing (which Company is in no way obligated to do), you will promptly reimburse Company for such excess upon demand and, without limiting Company's other rights and remedies, Company may deduct an amount equal to such excess from any monies otherwise payable to you or Artist hereunder. Artist's compensation for performing in each video (as opposed to your compensation with respect to the exploitation of such videos, which is provided elsewhere herein) will be limited to any minimum amounts required to be paid for such performances pursuant to any collective bargaining agreements pertaining thereto, provided, however, that Artist hereby waives any right to receive such compensation to the extent such right may be waived.

Contracts vary as to whether the artist will have any input into the time and place of production and/or the concept of the video. As a practical matter, however, the artist will generally be allowed to have input, even though the company may retain the final word.

If the record company chooses to authorize videos, it will want to ensure that the songwriter's publishing company will not create any obstacles to the recording and distribution of the video.

c.   *You will issue (or cause the music publishing companies having the right to do so to issue) (1) worldwide, perpetual synchronization licenses, and (2) perpetual licenses for public performance in the United States (to the extent that ASCAP and BMI are unable to issue same), to Company at no cost for the use of all Controlled Compositions in any promotional video effective as of the commencement of production of the applicable video (and your execution of this agreement constitutes the issuance of such licenses by any music publishing company that is owned or controlled by you, Artist or any Person owned or controlled by you or Artist). In the event that you fail to cause any such music publishing company to issue any such license to Company, or if Company is required to pay any fee to such music publishing company in order to obtain any such license for a promotional video, Company will have the right to deduct the amount of such license fee from any and all sums otherwise payable to you hereunder. Notwithstanding the foregoing, although the synchronization license is perpetual and*

> remains in effect, if the cost incurred with any such video is
> entirely recouped, then after such recoupment, and only with
> respect to prospective commercial uses of such Video, at your writ-
> ten request prior to Company's proposed exploitation, Company
> and you will negotiate in good faith with respect to compensation
> consistent with the then current Company standards, to be paid by
> Republic for such a synchronization license for the Controlled
> Compositions used in such video.

This provision ensures that, if the artist has retained any of his or her publishing, the publishing company will not charge any fees for the licensing of the
composition for videos, unless all costs are recouped.

S. Digital Performance Rights and Artist Web Sites

With the advent of the Internet and recent amendments to federal laws concerning the use of master recordings on the Web, many recording contracts
contain provisions related to artist's web sites and to the record company's
rights to "digitally perform" the masters created under the contract. These provisions are fairly recent (within the last five to six years), and vary widely in
concept and wording. However, the general rule is that the record company
with any presence on the Internet should own the Web site or limit the artist's
right to grant others rights in the Web site.

If the record company owns the Web site, it should allow the artist to maintain its own site, provided that the artist's site is not the "official" site. Also,
record company ownership will usually result in some division of the Web
site's revenue from banner ads, product sales, cross-linking agreements, etc. If
Livin' Large's contract with Groove Therapy provided that Livin' Large would
own the domain name Groove Therapy.com, the "official" Groove Therapy
web site, then Livin' Large and Groove Therapy might evenly divide the
income from advertisements placed on the site.

If, on the other hand, the artist retains the rights in their Web site, the artist
would generally promise to maintain a "first class" site. The artist would likely
not be permitted to assign the rights in the domain name to someone else and
would likely be restricted in what links they could include on their site.
Therefore, if Groove Therapy retained the rights in Groove Therapy.com,
Livin' Large would probably not want Groove Therapy to include a link to a
competing record label, a porn site, a music sharing web site, or the like.
Therefore, Livin' Large might require prior approval of all links included on
the site.

Furthermore, you should note that the record company owns the copyrights to the master recordings contained on the album. Therefore, if the artist intends to play its own music on its Web site, the agreement must provide a license to do so. The digital performance of sound recordings is governed by an extremely lengthy and complex piece of legislation that is beyond the scope of this discussion. Suffice it to say that, although the license is necessary in order for the artist to play sound clips, most provisions that address these licenses contain fairly complicated limitations and exceptions.

Conclusion

As you can see, there are many considerations in making a deal with a recording artist. A cautious record label should explore every possible avenue for recovering its investment, especially considering how many groups fail to sell significant numbers of records and considering the massive competition that exists in the marketplace. The recording and releasing of records is an expensive process that should not be agreed to without a firm agreement in place.

However the publishing is addressed in the recording agreement, an independent record label should have its own publishing company and should be prepared to make publishing deals. These agreements can originate from the record deal, which requires separate contracts with the record company's publisher, or can be made separately. In the next chapter, we will examine songwriter agreements between songwriters and the record company's publisher.

Form
Recording Artist Agreement

AGREEMENT made this____day of_____, by and between Livin' Large RECORDS, INC. (herein the "Company") and Fred, Bob and Joe p/k/a Groove Therapy, (herein referred to as "you").

In consideration of the mutual promises and covenants herein contained, the parties hereby agree as follows:

1. TERM

   a. The term hereof (the "Term") shall consist of an initial period (the "First Contract Period") of two (2) years plus the additional "Contract Periods", if any, by which such Term may be extended by Company's exercise of one or more of the options granted to Company below (unless otherwise extended or suspended as provided herein).

   b. You hereby irrevocably grant to Company two (2) consecutive options to extend the term for a Contract period. The options shall automatically be exercised unless Company gives you notice to the contrary at any time prior to the date that the then current Contract Period would otherwise expire.

   c. The First Contract Period shall commence on the date hereof and shall continue until the date eighteen (18) months after the Delivery to the Company of the Minimum Recording Commitment (of, if Company increases your recording commitment pursuant to paragraph 4 (b) hereof, eighteen (18) months after the Delivery to the Company of the additional recording commitment) for such Contract Period.

2. TERRITORY

The territory covered hereby (the "Territory") shall be the entire world.

3. RECORDING SERVICES

During the Term of the Agreement, you shall render to Company your exclusive services as a recording artist for the purpose of making Master Recordings and as otherwise set forth herein.

4. RECORDING COMMITMENT

a. During each Contract Period, you shall render your services to Company, in accordance with the terms and conditions hereof, in connection with the recording of sides sufficient to constitute one (1) long playing album (the "Minimum Recording Commitment") of not less than forty-five (45) minutes. The Minimum Recording Commitment for each period shall be Delivered, as defined herein, to Company within six (6) months following the commencement of the applicable contract period, unless Company, at its sole and absolute discretion, extends the period for Delivery as required or desired by Company.

b. Company shall have the right to increase your recording commitment in respect to any Contract Year; and you shall render to Company your exclusive services as a recording artist in connection with such additional number of Sides in excess of the Minimum Recording Commitment as Company may request from time to time. However, you shall not be obligated to perform hereunder for the recording of more than two (2) Albums (in the aggregate) during each Contract Year.

5. RECORDING PROCEDURE

a. In connection with Master Recordings to be made hereunder the selection of dates of recording and studio where recording is to take place, including the cost of recording therein, shall be mutually determined by you and Company provided that in the event of any dispute regarding such matters, Company's decision shall control.

b. Each Master Recording made hereunder shall be subject to Company's approval as "Satisfactory" (as defined herein) for the manufacture and sale of Phonograph Records. As used herein, Master Recordings shall be deemed "Satisfactory" if they contain first class vocal performances of a style and quality consistent with your previous recordings, and if (to the extent controlled in whole or in part by you) they are technically satisfactory for the manufacture and sale of phonograph records therefrom.

6. RECORDING COSTS

a. Company will pay all specifically approved Recording Costs in connection with Master Recordings made hereunder, all costs of all non-royalty instrumental, vocal and other personnel, and arrangements and copying incurred by Company hereunder, and all other amounts which are required to be paid by Company pursuant to any applicable law or any collective bargaining agreement between Company and any union representing persons who render services in connection with Master Recordings made hereunder.

b. In the event that Company's recording facility is used in connection with any Album hereunder, for purposes of determining recoupment of Recording Costs, Company's recording facility shall be billed out at Eighty Dollars ($80.00) per hour, which shall include engineering services provided by Company's in-house engineering staff. Subject to Company's consent, if Artist desires to use outside engineers and/or producers, the amounts which Company will allocate for such services shall be subject to Company's prior approval, and shall be deemed fully recoupable by Company from Artist royalties.

c. Subject to the provisions of Paragraph 7 below, all amounts described in Paragraph 6(a) above and/or Paragraph 13(l) below, plus all other amounts paid by Company representing expenses incurred in connection with the making of Master Recordings hereunder (i.e., the costs and expenses set forth in Paragraph 13(l) below,) are herein sometimes called "Recording Costs" and shall constitute Advances.

d. Nothing contained in this Agreement shall obligate Company to permit the continuation of any recording session to be held in connection with Master Recordings hereunder, if Company reasonably anticipates that the Master Recordings being recorded will not be Satisfactory.

7. ADVANCES

a. Company agrees to pay you an advance recoupable from all royalties hereunder in the sum of _____Dollars ($_____). Said Advance shall be payable upon execution of this Agreement.

b.   Any and all monies paid to you pursuant to this paragraph, as well as any and all other monies paid to you, or on your behalf, pursuant to or in connection with this Agreement (other than royalties paid pursuant to Paragraph 9 hereof), including Recording Costs, shall constitute Advances and shall be fully recoupable from Artist's royalties unless otherwise expressly agreed in writing by an authorized officer of Company.

8. GRANT OF RIGHTS

a.   All Master Recordings recorded hereunder from the inception of recording thereof, and all Phonograph Records manufactured there-from, together with the performances embodied thereon, shall be the sole property of Company throughout the world, free from any claims whatsoever by you or any other Person; and Company shall have the exclusive right to copyright such Master Recordings in its name as the owner and author thereof and to secure any and all renewals and extensions of such copyright. Solely for the purposes of any applicable copyright law, all Persons rendering services in connection with the recording of such Master Recordings shall be deemed "employees for hire" of Company.

b.   Without limiting the generality of the foregoing, Company and any Person authorized by Company shall have the unlimited right, throughout the world, to manufacture Phonograph Records by any method now or hereafter known, derived from the Master Recordings made hereunder, and to sell, market, transfer or otherwise deal in the same under any trademarks, trade names and labels, or to refrain from such manufacture, sale and dealing.

c.   Company and any Person authorized by Company each shall have the right, and may grant to others the right, to reproduce, print, publish, or disseminate in any medium your name, portraits, pictures, like-nesses and biographical material concerning you, as news or informa-tion, or for the purposes of trade, or for advertising purposes; provided, however, that no direct endorsement by you of any product or service shall be used without your prior written consent. During the Term of this Agreement, you shall not authorize any Party other than Company to use your name or likeness in connection with the advertising or sale of Phonograph Records. As used in this Agreement, "name" shall include any professional names or sobriquets.

9. ROYALTIES

Conditioned upon your full and faithful performance of all the material terms and conditions hereof, you shall be paid in connection with the Net Sales of Records consisting entirely of Masters hereunder and sold by Company or its Licensees, a royalty computed as set forth hereinbelow:

a. Fifteen Percent (15%) of the Royalty Base Price in connection with the Sale Through Normal Retail Channels in the United States of America of Phonograph Records in disc, tape, or other forms.

b. In respect of Master Recordings licensed or made available by Company for the manufacture, distribution or sale of Phonograph Records through broadcast or other advertisement utilizing key-outlet distributors or any similar method of operation, or through any record club, mail order or similar operation or for use in connection with so-called "premium" operation or for use on a particular Record that is intended for sale through customary retail trade channels, or licenses of Masters on a flat fee or cent rate, Company shall credit your royalty account with fifty percent (50%) of the net royalty actually received by Company from such third parties after deducting all applicable third party payments.

c. In respect of Phonograph Records sold and audio visual devices sold to educational institutions, libraries, to armed forces post exchanges, through television or telemarketing and in respect of Multiple Albums or Mid-Priced Records, the royalty payable to you shall be two-thirds (2/3) of the otherwise applicable royalty rate.

d. In respect of Budget Records, the royalty rate payable to you shall be one-half (1/2) the otherwise applicable royalty rate.

e. In respect of Phonograph Records sold by Company or its Licensees for distribution in the Territory of Canada, or licensed or otherwise furnished by Company or its Licensees to others for its manufacture or distribution in the Territory of Canada, the royalty rate payable to you therefor shall be eighty-five percent (85%) of the applicable basic royalty rate which would have been payable to you if such Records had been sold for distribution in the Untied States of America. In respect of Phonograph Records sold by Company or its Licensees for distribution outside of the United States of America other than in the Territory of Canada, or licensed or otherwise furnished by Company or its Licensees to others for its manufacture or distribution outside of the United States of America other than in the Territory of Canada, the royalty rate payable to you therefor shall be one-half (1/2) of the applicable basic royalty rate which would have been payable to you if such Records had been sold for distribution in the Untied States of America.

f.   i.   If Company licenses Videos or makes commercial use of such Videos embodying Artist's performances, the royalty payable by Company to you shall be one-half (1/2) of Company's net receipts derived therefrom after deducting any and all direct costs and/or third party payments in connection with the creation, manufacture, exploitation or use of the Videos from Artist's share of net receipts and an additional fee in lieu of any overhead or distribution of twenty-five percent (25%) of gross receipts. If any item of direct costs is attributable to receipts from such uses of Masters made hereunder and other master recordings, the amount of the expense item that will be deductible in computing the net receipts under this paragraph will be determined by apportionment.

     ii.   With respect to home video devices embodying Artist's performances, if Company manufactures and distributes such devices through its distributor, rather than licensing a third party to do so, the following shall apply in lieu of Paragraph 9(f)(i): on units sold for distribution in the United States of America, fifteen percent (15%) of the Royalty Base Price; and on units sold for distribution outside the United States of America, ten percent (10%) of the Royalty Base Price. Said royalties shall be calculated after deducting any third party payments required in connection with the sale of such devices including, without limitation, artist and producer royalties and copyright payments.

10. MISCELLANEOUS ROYALTY PROVISIONS

Notwithstanding anything to the contrary contained in Paragraph 9 hereof:

a.   i.   With respect to Phonograph Records embodying Master Recordings made hereunder, together with other master recordings, the royalty rate payable to you shall be computed by multiplying the royalty rate otherwise applicable by a fraction, the numerator of which is the number of Sides contained thereon embodying Master Recordings made hereunder and the denominator of which is the total number of Sides contained on such Record; and

ii. With respect to Phonograph Records embodying Master Recordings made hereunder which embody your performances, together with the performances of another artist(s) to whom Company is obligated to pay royalties in respect of the sale of Phonograph Records derived form such Master Recordings, the royalty rate to be used in determining the royalties payable to you shall be computed by multiplying the royalty rate otherwise applicable thereto by a fraction, the numerator of which shall be one and the denominator of which shall be the total number of recording artists (including you) whose performances are embodied on such Master Recording.

b. i. No royalties shall be payable to you in respect of Phonograph Records sold by Company or its Licensees until payment for such Records has been received by Company, or for Phonograph Records sold as cut-outs after the listing of such Records has been deleted from the catalog of Company or the particular Licensee, or for scrap at a salvage or close-out price, or for less than fifty (50%) percent of Company's or its Licensee's regular wholesale price for such Records, or in respect of Phonograph Records distributed for promotional purposes or Phonograph Records sold or distributed to radio stations or for use on transportation carriers and facilities to promote or stimulate the sale of Phonograph Records, or in respect of Phonograph Records sold or distributed as "free" or "no-charge" or "bonus" Records (whether or not intended for resale); and

ii. Notwithstanding anything to the contrary contained in Paragraph 10(b)(i) above, in respect of the sale by Company to its dealers or distributors of Phonograph Records subject to a discount or merchandising plan, the number of Records deemed to have been sold shall be determined by reducing the number of Records shipped by the percentage of discount granted, and if a discount is granted in the form of "free" or "no-charge" Records such "free" or "no-charge" Records shall not be deemed included in the number of Records sold.

c. No royalty shall be payable to you unless and until Company has recouped all Advances and all Recording Costs in connection with the Master Recordings produced hereunder from the royalties payable to you in respect of Net Sales of Phonograph Records embodying such Master Recordings, and after such recoupment, royalties shall be computed and paid to you only on those Records sold by Company or its Licensees after such recoupment.

d.   Company shall have the right to withhold a portion of your royalties as a reserve for returns and/or credits, which reserve shall be determined by Company in its reasonable judgment.

e.   The royalty rate applicable to a given Master Recording shall be the royalty rate specified herein for the Contract Year in which such Master Recording was recorded.

11. ROYALTY ACCOUNTING

a.   Company shall compute royalties payable to you hereunder as of June 30th and December 31st for each preceding six (6) month period during which Records as to which royalties are payable hereunder are sold, and shall use its best efforts to render a statement and pay such royalties, less any unrecouped Advances and any other permissible offsets prior to each succeeding September 30 and March 31st, respectively. Company may deduct from any royalty or other payment due to you under this Agreement any amount you may owe Company under this Agreement and/or any other agreement between you and Company or its affiliates, including products purchased under this Agreement.

b.   Royalties for Records sold for distribution outside of the United States of America (the "foreign sales") shall be computed in the national currency in which Company is paid by its Licensees and shall be paid to you at the same rate of exchange at which Company is paid. For accounting purposes, foreign sales shall be deemed to occur in the same semi-annual accounting periods in which Company's Licensees account to Company therefor. If Company is unable, for reasons beyond its control, to receive payment for such sales in United States Dollars in the United States of America, royalties therefor shall not be credited to your account during the continuance of such inability; if any accounting rendered to you hereunder during the continuance of such inability requires the payment of royalties to you, Company will, at your request and if Company is able to do so, deposit such royalties to your credit in such foreign currency in a foreign depository, at your expense.

c. At any time within one (1) year after any royalty statement is rendered to you hereunder, you shall have the right to give Company written notice of your intention to examine Company's books and records with respect to such statement. Such examination shall be commenced within three (3) months after the date of such notice, at your sole cost and expense, by any certified public accountant or attorney designated by you, provided he is not then engaged in an outstanding examination of Company's books and records on behalf of a person other than you. Such examination shall be made during Company's usual business hours at the place where Company maintains the books and records which relate to you and which are necessary to verify the accuracy of the statement or statements specified in your notice to Company and your examination shall be limited to the foregoing. Your right to inspect Company's books and records shall be only as set forth in this Paragraph 11(c) and Company shall have no obligation to produce such books and records more than once with respect to each statement rendered to you.

d. Unless notice is given to Company as provided in Paragraph 11(c) hereof, each royalty statement rendered to you shall be final, conclusive and binding on you and shall constitute an account stated. You shall be foreclosed from maintaining any action, claim or proceeding against Company in any forum or tribunal with respect to any statement or accounting rendered hereunder unless such action, claim or proceeding is commenced against Company within one (1) year after completion of the examination set forth in subparagraph 11(c).

e. You acknowledge that Company's books and records contain confidential trade information. Neither you nor your representatives will communicate to others or use on behalf of any other person any facts or information obtained as a result of such examination of Company's books and records.

f. Notwithstanding anything to the contrary contained herein, if any accounting provisions contained in any distribution agreement between Company and its distributor contains terms more restrictive than those contained herein, the applicable provisions hereof shall be deemed amended to conform with the distribution agreement.

12. WARRANTIES, REPRESENTATIONS, RESTRICTIONS AND INDEM-
    NITIES

   a.   You warrant and represent that:

       i.   You are under no disability, restriction or prohibition, whether contractual or otherwise, with respect to your right to enter into this Agreement and your right to grant the rights granted to Company hereunder, to perform each and every term and provision hereof, and to record each and every Composition hereunder;

      ii.   Company shall not be required to make any payments of any nature for, or in connection with, the acquisition, exercise or exploitation of rights by Company pursuant to this Agreement, except as specifically provided in this Agreement;

    iii.   You are or will become and will remain to the extent necessary to enable the performance of this Agreement, a member in good standing of all labor unions or guilds, membership in which may be lawfully required for the performance of your services hereunder;

    iv.   Neither the "Materials" nor any use of the Materials by Company will violate any law or infringe upon any rights of any Person. "Materials" as used in this subparagraph means any musical, artistic and literary materials, ideas and other intellectual properties, furnished by you and contained in or used in connection with any Recordings made hereunder or the packaging, sale, distribution, advertising, publicizing or other exploitation thereof;

     v.   There are now in existence no prior recorded performances by you unreleased within the United States of America and elsewhere in the world.

    vi.   All of your representations and warranties shall be true and correct upon execution hereof and upon delivery of each Master Recording hereunder, and shall remain in effect in perpetuity. Company's acceptance of Master Recordings or other materials hereunder shall not constitute a waiver of any of your representations, warranties or agreements in respect thereof.

vii. In connection with each recording session conducted hereunder, you will comply with the following procedures required by United States immigration law:

    a. Before any individual renders services in connection with the recording of any Master hereunder (including, without limitation, each background instrumentalist, background vocalist, producer and engineer):

        1. You will require each such individual to complete and sign the EMPLOYEE INFORMATION AND VERIFICATION ("employee section") of a U.S. Immigration and Naturalization Service ("INS") Employment Eligibility Certificate ("Form I-9"), unless you have already obtained (and retained) such certificate from that individual within the past three years;

        2. You will complete and sign the EMPLOYER REVIEW AND VERIFICATION ("employer section") of each such certificate; and

        3. You will attach copies of the documents establishing identity and employment eligibility that you examine in accordance with the instructions in the employer section.

    b. You will not permit any such Person who fails to complete the employee section (or to furnish you with the required documentation) to render any services in connection with Recordings made under this agreement.

    c. You will deliver the employee and employer certificates (with copies of the necessary documents attached) to Company within seventy-two (72) hours after the conclusion of the session concerned.

    d. You will comply with any revised or additional verification and documentation procedures required by the INS in the future.

b. i. During the Term of this Agreement, you will not enter into any agreement which would interfere with the full and prompt performance of your obligations hereunder, and you will not perform or render any services for the purpose of making Phonograph Records or Master Recordings for any person other than Company. After the expiration of the Term of this Agreement, for any reason whatsoever, you will not perform any Composition which shall have been recorded hereunder for any person other than Company for the purpose of making Phonograph Records or Master Recordings prior to the date five (5) years subsequent to the expiration date of the Term of the Agreement; and

ii.   You will not at any time record, manufacture, distribute or sell, or authorize or knowingly permit your performances to be recorded by any party for any purpose without an express written agreement prohibiting the use of such Recording on Phonograph Records in violation of the foregoing restrictions.

c.   In the event that you shall become aware of any unauthorized recording, manufacture, distribution or sale by any third party contrary to the foregoing re-recording restrictions, you shall notify Company thereof and shall cooperate with Company in the event that Company commences any action or proceeding against such third party.

d.   Your services hereunder are unique and extraordinary, and the loss thereof cannot be adequately compensated in damages, and Company shall be entitled to injunctive relief to enforce the provisions of this Agreement.

e.   You will at all times indemnify and hold harmless Company and any Licensee of Company from and against any and all claims, damages, liabilities, costs and expenses, including legal expenses and reasonable counsel fees, arising out of any alleged breach or actual breach by you of any warranty, representation or agreement made by you herein. You will reimburse Company and/or its Licensees on demand for any payment made at any time after the date hereof in respect of any liability or claim in respect of which Company or its Licensees are entitled to be indemnified. Upon the making or filing of any such claim, action or demand, Company shall be entitled to withhold from any amounts payable under this Agreement such amounts as are reasonably related to the potential liability at issue. You shall be notified of any such claim, action or demand and shall have the right, at your own expense, to participate in the defense thereof with counsel of your own choosing; provided, however, that Company's decision in connection with the defense of any such claim, action or demand shall be final.

f.   You shall execute and deliver to Company, upon Company's request therefor, a form of artist inducement and guarantee letter as may be required by Company's distributor. If you shall fail or refuse to execute and deliver any such inducement letter promptly following Company's request therefor, you hereby appoint Company your true and lawful attorney-in-fact to execute such inducement letter in your name and on your behalf. Such power of attorney is irrevocable and is coupled with and interest.

13. DEFINITIONS

As used in this Agreement, the following terms shall have the meanings set forth below:

a. *Advance*—amount recoupable by Company from royalties to be paid to you or on your behalf pursuant to this Agreement or any other agreement between you and Company or its affiliates.

b. *Album*—one (1) twelve-inch, 33-1/3 rpm Record, or the equivalent thereof, embodying thereon not less than eight (8) Sides, whether or not released, which are recorded in connection with a specific album project, that contains at least forty-five (45) minutes of playing time.

c. *Composition*—a single musical composition, irrespective of length, including all spoken words and bridging passages and including a medley.

d. *Container Charge*—(i) with respect to vinyl Phonograph Records, twenty percent (20%) of the applicable Wholesale Selling Price of such Phonograph Records; and (ii) with respect to Phonograph Records in other configurations, including without limitation cassette tapes, compact discs, videos, DVDs, CD ROMs and CD Singles, twenty-five percent (25%) of the applicable Wholesale Selling Price of such Phonograph Records; and (iii) with respect to 7-inch Single Phonograph Records contained in non-standard color sleeves, twenty percent (20%) of the applicable Wholesale Selling Price of such Phonograph Records.

e. *Controlled Composition*—a composition written, owned or controlled, in whole or in party, by you and/or any Person in which you have a direct or indirect interest.

f. *Delivered* or *Delivery*—the actual receipt by Company of Master Recordings, fully mixed and edited and otherwise in the proper form for the production of parts necessary for the manufacture of records, Satisfactory to Company and ready for Company's manufacture of

Phonograph Records, and all necessary licenses, consents and approvals.

g. *Licensees*—includes, without limitation, any distributor and all subsidiaries, wholly or partly owned, and other divisions of Company and any of Company's licensees.

h. *Master Recordings*—each and every Recording of sound, whether or not coupled with a visual image, by any method and on any other substance or material, whether now or hereafter known, which is used or useful in the recording, production and/or manufacture of Phonograph Records.

i. *Net Sales*—Ninety percent (90%) of gross sales less returns and credits of any nature.

j. *Person* and *Party*—any individual, corporation, partnership, association or other entity or organized group of persons or legal successors or representatives of the foregoing.

k. *Records, Phonograph Records* and *Recordings*—all forms of reproductions, now or hereafter known, manufactured or distributed primarily for home use, school use, juke box use, or use in means of transportation, embodying (i) sound alone; or (ii) sound coupled with visual images, e.g. "sight and sound" devices.

l. *Recording Costs*—all amounts representing direct expenses incurred by the Company in connection with the recording of Masters hereunder, including without limitation, payments to vocalists, musicians, arrangers, sketchers, conductors, orchestrators, producers, contractors and copyists in connection with the recording of the Master Recordings made hereunder, together with payroll taxes thereon, payments based on payroll to any labor organization or designee thereof, advances and/or fees to the producer of the Master Recordings (it being understood that no separate fee or advance shall be payable to you for any producing services you provide in connection with the Master Recordings), the cost of cartage and rental of instruments for such recording sessions, studio cost, in connection with the Company's facilities and personnel or otherwise, transportation costs, hotel and living expenses incurred in connection with the preparation and attendance of performers, the individual producers, musicians and other essential personnel at recording sessions, tapes, editing and other similar costs in connection with the production of the final tape master and the lacquer master, and all other costs generally and customarily recognized as recording costs in the industry.

m. *Royalty Base Price*—the applicable suggested Wholesale Selling Price of Phonograph Records less all taxes, distribution expenses and applicable Container Charge.

n. *Sales Through Normal Retail Channels in the United States of America*—sales other than as described in subparagraphs 9(b) through (f).

o. *Side*—a Recording of sufficient playing time to constitute one (1) Side of a 45 rpm Record, but not less than two and one-half (2-½) minutes of continuous sound.

p. *Single* or *Single Record*—one (1) 7-inch or 12-inch Record embodying thereon not more than three (3) Sides.

q. *Videos*—Films or videotapes featuring your performances of Compositions embodied on Master Recordings recorded hereunder.

r. *Wholesale Selling Price*—with respect to Records sold to distributors in the United States of America and with respect to Records sold for distribution outside of the United States of America, the Wholesale Selling Price of such Records, in, at Company's election, the country of manufacture, the United States of America or the country of sale.

14. SUSPENSION AND TERMINATION

a. If at any time you fail, except solely for Company's refusal without cause to allow you to perform, to fulfill your recording commitment within the times set forth herein, then, without limiting Company's rights, Company shall have the option, exercisable at any time by notice to you, to (i) terminate this Agreement without any further obligation to you as to unrecorded Master Recordings, or (ii) to suspend Company's obligations to you hereunder during the period of default, and/or (iii) to extend the expiration date of the current period of the Term for the period of the default plus such additional time as is necessary so that Company shall have no less than one hundred twenty (120) days after completion of your recording commitment within which to exercise its option, if any, for the next following contract year.

b. If, in respect of any contract year of the Term of this Agreement, Company fails, without cause, to allow you to fulfill your Minimum Recording Commitment within nine (9) months following the commencement of any Contract Period and if, within thirty (30) days after the expiration of such nine (9) month period you shall notify Company of your desire to fulfill such Minimum Recording Commitment, then Company shall permit you to fulfill said Minimum Recording Commitment by notice to you to such effect within sixty (60) days of Company's receipt of your notice. Should Company fail to give such notice, you shall have the option within thirty (30) days after the expiration of said sixty (60) day period to give Company notice that you wish to terminate the Term of this Agreement; on receipt by Company of such notice, the Term of this Agreement shall terminate and all parties will be deemed to have fulfilled all of the obligations hereunder, except those obligations which survive the end of the Term (e.g., warranties, re-recording restrictions and obligations to pay royalties). In the event you fail to give Company either notice within the period specified therefor, Company shall be under no obligation to you for failing to permit you to fulfill such Minimum Recording Commitment or otherwise.

c. If, because of an act of God, inevitable accident, fire, lockout, strike or other labor dispute, riot or civil commotion, act of public enemy, enactment, rule, order or act of any government or governmental instrumentality (whether federal, state, local or foreign), failure of technical facilities, failure or delay of transportation facilities, illness or incapacity of any performer or producer, or other cause of a similar or different nature not reasonably within Company's control, Company is materially hampered in the recording, manufacture, distribution or sale of Records, or Company's normal business operations become commercially impractical, then, without limiting Company's rights, Company shall have the option by giving you notice to suspend the Term of this Agreement for the duration of any such contingency plus such additional time as is necessary so that Company shall have no less than thirty (30) days after the cessation of such contingency in which to exercise its option, if any, for the next following option period. Any such extension of the then current Contract Year due to any cause set forth in this Paragraph 14(c) which involves only Company shall be limited to a period of six (6) months.

d. You agree that Company may suspend payment of any amounts due you under this Agreement, including without limitation artist royalties, songwriter royalties and publisher royalties, if you breach any warranty or representation made herein or if you fail to deliver any documents or any information requested by Company that is necessary to secure all rights for Company in each Album. You agree that such suspension may continue until you have complied with Company's requests and/or cured any breach hereunder.

15. ASSIGNMENT

Company may assign this Agreement to any third party or to any subsidiary, affiliated or controlling corporation or to any Person owning or acquiring a substantial portion of the stock or assets of Company. Company may also assign its rights hereunder to any of its Licensees to the extent necessary or advisable in Company's sole discretion to implement the license granted. You may not assign this Agreement or any of your rights hereunder.

16. NOTICES

Except as otherwise specifically provided herein, all notices hereunder shall be in writing and shall be given by registered or certified mail at the respective addresses hereinabove set forth, or such other address or addresses as may be designated by either party. Such notices shall be deemed given when mailed, except that notice of change of address shall be effective only from the date of its receipt.

17. CONFIDENTIALITY

The terms of this contract are confidential and neither the Company and/or its principals nor you and/or your principals or any agent of either party shall divulge the contents of this contract to any Person without the prior written consent of both parties to this contract. In the event of a breach of this contractual provision it shall not be assumed that either party suffered damages.

18. MISCELLANEOUS

a. This Agreement contains the entire understanding of the parties hereto relating to the subject matter hereof and cannot be changed or terminated by you except by an instrument signed by an officer of

Company. A waiver by either party of any term or condition of this Agreement in any instance shall not be deemed or construed as a waiver of such term or condition for the future, or of any subsequent breach thereof. All remedies, rights, undertakings, obligations, and agreements contained in this Agreement shall be cumulative and none of them shall be in limitation of any other remedy, right, undertaking, obligation or agreement of either party.

b.   It is understood and agreed that in entering into this Agreement, and in rendering services pursuant thereto, you have, and shall have, the status of an independent contractor and nothing herein contained shall contemplate or constitute you as Company's employee or agent.

c.   Those provisions of any applicable collective bargaining agreement between Company and any labor organization which are required, by the terms of such agreement, to be included in this Agreement shall be deemed incorporated herein.

d.   No breach of this Agreement on the part of Company shall be deemed material, unless you shall have given Company notice of such breach and Company shall fail to discontinue the practice complained of (if practice of Company is the basis of the claim of breach) or otherwise cure such breach, within sixty (60) days after receipt of such notice, if such breach is reasonably capable of being fully cured within such sixty (60) day period, or, if such breach is not reasonably capable of being fully cured within such sixty (60) day period, if Company commences to cure such breach within such sixty (60) day period and proceeds with reasonable diligence to complete the curing of such breach.

e.   This Agreement has been entered into in the State of _____, and the validity, interpretation and legal effect of this Agreement shall be governed by the laws of the State of _____ applicable to contracts entered into and performed entirely within the State of _____. The _____ courts only, will have jurisdiction of any controversies regarding this Agreement; and, any action or other proceeding that involves such a controversy will be brought in the courts located within the State of _____ and not elsewhere. Any process in any action or proceeding commenced in the courts of the State of _____ arising out of any such claim, dispute, or disagreement, may, among other methods, be served upon you by delivering or mailing the same, via registered or certified mail, addressed to you at the address first above written or such other address as you may designate pursuant to Paragraph 16 hereof. Any such delivery or mail service shall be deemed to have the same force and effect as personal service within the State of _____.

f. If any part of this Agreement shall be determined to be invalid or unenforceable by a court of competent jurisdiction or by any other legally constituted body having jurisdiction to make such determination, the remainder of this Agreement shall remain in full force and effect.

19. GROUP

The terms of this Paragraph 19 shall be effective in the event that you are comprised of more than one (1) individual:

a. Your obligations under the terms of this Agreement are joint and several and all references to you shall include all members comprising you jointly and each member comprising you individually, unless otherwise specifically provided herein.

b. You represent and warrant that you are the sole owner of any and every group name now used or hereafter adopted by you insofar as rights of ownership can be acquired in a group name; that no other person or persons have the right to use said group name or to authorize or license its use in connection with Records; that you have the full right and authority to grant to Company all of the rights to use said group name as is contemplated in this Agreement.

c. Any breach of this Agreement by any of the persons comprising you shall be deemed to be a breach by all of the persons comprising the you.

d. If any member comprising you shall cease to perform as a member of the group, the following provisions shall apply:

   i. You shall promptly notify Company thereof and such leaving member shall be replaced by a new member, and such new member shall be subject to Company's approval. Such approved new member shall thereafter be deemed substituted as a party to this Agreement in the place of such leaving member and shall automatically be bound by all the terms and conditions of this Agreement. Upon Company's request, you will cause any such new member to execute and deliver to Company such documents as Company, in its judgment, may deem necessary or advisable to effectuate the foregoing sentence. Thereafter, the leaving member shall no longer be required to render his recording services hereunder as a member of the group, but you (and such leaving member individually) shall continue to be bound by the other provisions of this Agreement, including, without limitation, subparagraph (d)(iv) below;

ii. Notwithstanding anything to the contrary contained herein, Company shall have the right to terminate the Term of this Agreement by written notice given to you at any time prior to the expiration of ninety (90) days after Company's receipt of your said notice to Company. In the event of such termination, all of the members comprising you shall be deemed leaving members as of the date of such termination notice, and subparagraph (d)(iv) below shall be applicable to you;

iii, Each leaving member hereby relinquishes all of his rights in the group name to the remaining members of the group; and

iv. Company shall have, and you hereby grant to Company, an option to engage the exclusive services of such leaving member as a recording artist ("Leaving Member Option"). Such Leaving Member Option may be exercised by Company by notice at any time prior to the expiration of ninety (90) days after the date of (A) Company's receipt of your notice provided for in subparagraph (d)(i) above, or (B) Company's termination notice pursuant to subparagraph (d)(ii) above, as the case may be. If Company exercises such Leaving Member Option, the leaving member concerned shall be deemed to be bound by a new exclusive recording artist agreement (the "New Agreement") that contains the same terms and conditions as are contained herein, except that (i) the Commencement date of the New Agreement shall be the date Company exercises its Leaving Member Option, (ii) the Minimum Recording Commitment shall not exceed one (1) Album per Contract Year, and (iii) and the basic royalty rate shall be the basic royalty rate payable pursuant to this Agreement and (iv) no Advances otherwise payable to you shall be payable to the leaving member in the New Agreement.

20. MERCHANDISING RIGHTS

You hereby grant to Company and its Licensees the exclusive right, throughout the World, to use and authorize the use of your name, portraits, pictures, likenesses and biographical material, either alone or in conjunction with other elements, in connection with the sale, lease, licensing or other disposition of merchandising rights. For the rights granted by you to Company in this paragraph, Company shall pay to you a royalty of twenty-five (25%) percent of Company's net royalty receipts derived from the exploitation of such rights, after deducting all costs and third party payments relating thereto; and such royalty shall be accounted to you in the manner otherwise provided herein.

21. CO-PUBLISHING

You hereby irrevocably and absolutely assign, convey and set over to Company and/or Company's publishing designee a fifty (50%) right, title and interest (including the worldwide copyright and all extensions and renewals of such copyrights) in and to each and every Controlled Composition that is recorded hereunder. You agree to execute and deliver to Company (or Company's affiliated music publishing company or to any other publishing company designated by Company), a separate Songwriter's Agreement in respect to each Controlled Composition subject to the provisions of this paragraph, in the form of Exhibit "A" attached hereto and made a part hereof by this reference. All the terms and conditions of said Songwriter's Agreement shall govern the respective rights and obligations of the parties with respect to such Controlled Compositions. If you shall fail to promptly execute such Songwriter's Agreement, you hereby irrevocably grant to Company a power of attorney to execute said agreement in your name.

22. MECHANICAL ROYALTIES

a. You hereby grant Company, its distributors and its licensees, an irrevocable license under copyright to reproduce each Controlled Composition on records and to distribute them throughout the Territory.

b. Any assignment made of the ownership of copyrights, or of the rights to license or administer the use of any Controlled Compositions, shall be subject to the terms and provisions hereof.

c.   If any Album made under this Agreement contains compositions that are not Controlled Compositions, you will obtain licenses covering those compositions on terms no less favorable to Company than those contained in the then-current standard mechanical license issued by The Harry Fox Agency, Inc. You will also cause to be issued to Company licenses to reproduce each non-Controlled Composition on records distributed in the rest of the universe on terms as favorable as those generally prevailing in the country concerned.

d.   You hereby agree to grant Company a mechanical license to reproduce each Controlled Composition for a royalty equal to seventy five percent (75%) of the minimum applicable statutory rate in effect in the United States or other applicable country on the date of the first commercial release of the record. If the copyright law of any given country does not provide for a minimum compulsory rate, but the major record companies and major music publishers in such country have agreed to a mechanical license rate (the "Agreed Rate"), you agree to grant Company a mechanical license to reproduce each Controlled Composition for a royalty equal to seventy five percent (75%) of the Agreed Rate in effect on the date of the first commercial release of the record. With respect to non-Controlled Compositions you shall use your best efforts to assist Company in obtaining similar terms from the copyright owner.

e.   Subject to subparagraph 22(f), and notwithstanding anything else to the contrary contained herein, the maximum combined rate for all Compositions on each Album shall not exceed ten (10) times seventy five percent (75%) of such minimum applicable statutory or Agreed Rate ("Mechanical Royalty Cap"). To the extent that Company is required to pay mechanical royalties in excess of such Mechanical Royalty Cap, Company may deduct such excess from any and all monies otherwise payable to Artist hereunder.

f.   Notwithstanding anything to the contrary contained herein, if any mechanical license provisions for Controlled Compositions contained in any distribution agreement between Company and its distributor contains terms more restrictive than those contained herein, the applicable provisions hereof shall be deemed amended to conform with the distribution agreement.

23. VIDEO RELEASES

a. Company, in its sole discretion, shall have the right to require you to perform at such times and places as Company designates for the production of Videos. Company shall be the exclusive owner throughout the world and in perpetuity of the Videos, if any, and all rights therein, including all copyrights and renewal of copyrights, and shall have all of the rights with respect thereto which are set forth in Paragraph 8 above, including without limitation the right (but not the obligation) to use and exploit Videos in any and all forms.

b. All sums paid by Company in connection with the production of Videos shall constitute Advances to you that are recoupable from fifty percent (50%) of all record royalties payable to you under this Agreement and one hundred percent (100%) of all video royalties payable to you hereunder.

PART TWO

PUBLISHING AGREEMENTS

Chapter 2

The Non-Exclusive Songwriter:
It's All About the Publishing

The artist has been "signed." Now what? As we discussed in Chapter 1, assuming that the artist writes his or her own material, the publishing is a major source of income. If the artist has agreed to assign all publishing as part of the recording artist agreement, then the record company will need to have its publisher enter into a songwriting agreement with the songwriter. Even if the artist only assigns a portion of the publishing to the record company's publisher, the artist must still enter into a songwriter agreement with his or her own publisher prior to making co-publishing arrangements with the record company's publisher.

So what does a publisher do, exactly? A publisher is responsible for a number of tasks. These tasks include: filing copyright registrations, filing registrations with performance rights societies; granting licenses to others who wish to record the composition, print sheet music, make a music video, etc.; collecting income and distributing it to the songwriters; and promoting the composition in an attempt to get others to use the song. As we discussed in Chapter 1, it is important to understand that the artist and the songwriter play separate roles, even where they are the same people. They have different jobs, take different rights, and realize different income. This can be a very complicated area in which to work, but it is *very* important to understand the difference, especially considering that so many artists write their own material. Because the distinction is so important, let's reexamine our example from Chapter 1.

Fred, Joe and Bob write their own music and perform their music as the rock band known as Groove Therapy. Therefore, Fred, Joe and Bob have two distinct jobs—they are songwriters and they are performers. As we discussed in Chapter 1, these two income streams should not be commingled. If, therefore, Fred, Joe and Bob decide to "cover" a song written by another songwriter, then they will only be paid as artists—the songwriter royalties will go else-where. The reverse is true, as well. If Fred, Joe and Bob write a song that is recorded by another band, then Fred, Joe and Bob will receive songwriter roy-alties but not artist royalties. This sounds fairly simple, right? However, it is amazing how often the distinction is lost when the recording artist and the songwriter are the same person (or people). For purposes of this chapter, just keep in mind that we are talking about songwriting, and not performing.

If a recording artist signs with a record company who assumes any of the publishing rights, (and many do) then there will be an agreement assigning some or all of the publishing to the record company's affiliated publishing company. If not, the artist (or, for that matter, the independent songwriter) may do anything with the publishing rights that he or she chooses. This could include a separate deal with a publisher or self-publishing. Because of the administrative tasks associated with publishing (filings with the copyright office and the performance rights society and issuing licenses) and because of the limited ability that many individuals have to promote their own music, most songwriters choose to assign some of their publishing rights to a pub-lisher, if possible.

Songwriters can either assign each song on an individual basis (a non-exclusive songwriter agreement) or assign all publishing rights for all songs they write within a particular time frame (an exclusive songwriter agreement).

A non-exclusive songwriter agreement is fairly simple, especially as com-pared to the recording artist agreement. In essence, the agreement will assign all the publishing rights and retain all songwriter royalties. This also involves a transfer of the copyright ownership. You should note that, where a songwriter wishes to retain some or all of the copyright, a different approach is required. For instance, where a songwriter wants to retain half ownership in the song, the writer would assign half of the copyright to his or her own publisher and half to the publisher with whom he or she wants to make a deal. This is the co-publishing arrangement. Generally, this is accomplished by assigning all rights to the songwriter's publisher, then having that publisher sign a co-publisher agreement that transfers half of the rights. Naturally, the more ownership a songwriter expects to keep, while contracting out the work, the more clout a songwriter must have.

To illustrate these concepts, let's return to our example. John, a songwriter, writes a song that catches the attention of an executive at Livin' Large records. Livin' Large believes that the song would be a good addition to Groove Therapy's next album. John is fairly new to the songwriting business, and is unsigned at this point. Livin' Large agrees to pitch the song to Groove Therapy if John will grant their publishing affiliate, Uptown Publishing, all of his publishing rights. If John agrees, Uptown would present John with a Non-Exclusive Songwriter Agreement. The Non-Exclusive Songwriter Agreement would assign all of the rights to this single song to Uptown, but John would retain all ownership in his other compositions.

A. Grant of Rights

The agreement will usually start by assigning all rights to the publisher:

> *Composer assigns to Publisher, in perpetuity, all of his worldwide rights in the Composition, including without limitation, the title, words, and music thereof: all copyrights with respect thereto and the right to secure any extensions and renewals in the same and in any arrangements and adaptations thereof: and all other rights, which now or hereafter may exist at law or by agreement relating thereto. Composer irrevocably appoints Publisher, or any of its officers, his attorney, empowered to sign any instruments which Publisher may deem necessary to vest itself, its successors, assigns, and licensees, and of the rights referred to herein. Publisher may for the term of this Agreement use throughout the world Composer's name and likeness in connection with the use of the Composition, including without limitation printed versions thereof, and in connection with publicity and advertising concerning Publisher. Publisher may make arrangements, adaptations, translations and dramatizations of the Composition, and add new lyrics in a language other than English to the music of the Composition. Publisher shall collect all income earned by the Composition.*

This provision transfers the copyright in the work to the publisher and grants the publisher the right to collect all income, including the songwriting portion (although the next clause provides an exception to this grant). It also gives the publisher the right to use the songwriter's name, photograph, biographical information and the like, in order to advertise and promote the music.

B. Compensation

The publishing income is one half of the total income earned for any given composition. Therefore, considering that the publisher will be collecting all income produced by the song, the publisher must turn 50% of the total over to the songwriter, representing the "songwriter's share."

> *Publisher shall pay Composer fifty percent (50%) of all net sums actually received in the United States by Publisher and all allocable to the Composition for mechanical rights, print rights, synchronization rights and for any other use or exploitation of the Composition anywhere in the world: provided, however, Composer shall collect his public performance royalties throughout the world directly from his own affiliated performing rights society and shall have no claim whatsoever against Publisher for the "publisher's share" (as such term is commonly understood in the worldwide music industry) of any royalties received by Publisher from any performing rights society.*

Alternative clauses may quote an exact rate for certain uses (such as $0.06 for sale of sheet music) and 50% for any uses not otherwise spelled out. However, mechanical (recording) and synchronization (video) income is always split 50/50.

The exception noted above lies in the performance income—that is, the income derived from public performance of the song, including live performances, radio and television performances, etc., and paid by the performance rights societies (ASCAP, BMI, and SESAC). The writer is to collect the songwriter's share of the performance income directly from the society, rather than from the publisher. The publisher will likewise collect the publisher's share and will owe none of it to the songwriter.

C. Accounting

Publishing companies, like record companies, account at different intervals. A few account monthly but most account quarterly or, as here, every six months.

> *Publisher shall render royalty statements to Composer at least twice per year, but only for accounting periods in which royalties accrue. Statements will be accompanied by appropriate payments, if any. A Certified Public Accountant or attorney on Composer's behalf may examine the books of Publisher pertaining to the Composition during Publisher's usual business hours and upon thirty (30) days prior notice. Said books relating to activities and receipts during any accounting period may be examined as aforesaid only once and only during the two (2) year period following issuance of the statement for said accounting period. The supporting documents for any statement may be examined*

only once by Composer. If Composer does not institute a lawsuit within one (1) year of conducting an audit, then Composer shall forever be barred from making a claim as to the audited statement.

Most publishers will not render an accounting if no royalties accrue. For the publisher, this is the best practice because it reduces expenses for compositions that are not making money.

This clause also allows the songwriter to audit the publisher's records, with certain restrictions. Similar to recording agreements, there are usually limitations as to who may conduct an examination, how long a composer has to contest any given statement (from 6 months to 3 years), how many times the composer may examine any given record (usually only once), and how long after an examination the composer may bring suit, if necessary (usually 1 to 3 years).

Biz note: The importance of proper accountings cannot be overstressed, especially in the arena of songwriter/publisher royalties. As we discussed in chapter 1, artists frequently remain unrecouped for the duration of the record, and, although there must still be an accounting, the record company does not end up having to pay royalties. This is not true when it comes to songwriter/publisher royalties, and publishers who do not account and do not pay songwriter royalties, aside from being in breach of their contract, frequently find themselves saddled with an audit. Even though the audit is at the songwriter's expense, that only applies to the copying of documents and the payment of the auditor. The publisher still must pay his own CPA or attorney to review the documents, remove anything that the songwriter is not entitled by contract to see (such as sales for other songwriters), and prepare the publisher's own accounting—if the publisher chooses not to have his representative prepare the accounting for the audit period, then when the auditor comes back with a figure, the publisher has no clue whether that figure is correct and may end up overpaying. The price tag for an audit preparation for a multi-year period can run well into the five digit range, as opposed to a regularly scheduled accounting, which is much less expensive. It is much less costly to issue accountings on the front end than to defend the failure to do so on the back end.

D. Warranties

A warranty is a guarantee by the composer that things are as he or she says they are.

a. *Composer warrants that the Composition is an original work, cre-*
    ated solely by Composer, and will not infringe any copyright or vio-
    late or interfere with any interest, whether contractual, statutory,
    or otherwise, of any third party. Composer shall indemnify
    Publisher, its assigns, licensees and employees from any and all lia-
    bility or claims including reasonable outside attorneys fees and
    court costs arising out of or related to any claim inconsistent with
    any warranty or representation, express or implied, made by
    Composer herein.

The songwriter has to guarantee that the song was written by him or her and that there are no authors or other owners that the publisher does not know about. If it turns out later that there are, then the songwriter must pay back the publisher for any costs incurred because of the faulty guarantee. It is extremely common for a songwriter to be sued over a song, either because the songwriter supposedly copied someone else's work or because the songwriter supposedly forgot to mention a co-writer. The publisher does not want to incur expenses if the songwriter has a fight with a former acquaintance over creative matters.

For instance, I have been involved in several cases where a band was sued by a disgruntled former band member. In one particular case, although the band insisted that the former band member had no creative input whatsoever, the former band member just as strongly insisted otherwise. The former band member, therefore, sued the individual band members (including a member that joined the band after the former member's departure), the band as a whole, the band's publishing company, the record company, the record company's publishing company, the company that printed the sheet music, the distributors and anyone else that had had anything to do with the band's album. As these matters often do, the case continued for a very long time and costs for all parties were very high. Win or lose, the publisher stood to lose a great deal of money just in attorney's fees. Therefore, because the publisher has no control over the songwriter's compositions or co-writers, the publisher will always look to the songwriter for reimbursement of any costs when disputes arise.

b. *Publisher, at its discretion, may employ attorneys and institute or*
    defend any claim or action either in Composer's name, and take
    any necessary proper steps to protect the right, title and interest of
    Publisher in and to the Composition and in that connection to set-
    tle, compromise or in any other manner dispose of any such claim,

> *action or judgment that may be rendered. Notwithstanding the foregoing, Composer may, through legal counsel of Composer's choice, assume control of any dispute. Publisher will not incur any costs payable by Composer without Composer's consent.*

If there are any problems with the compositions that require legal attention, the publisher will have the right to take care of them. For instance, if Uptown hears Ray's new song, "Nuts," and it sounds a lot like Fred, Joe and Bob's song, "Cashews," Uptown would be able to hire attorneys and file suit for infringement. Of course, Fred, Joe and Bob could hire lawyers and take charge of the case, but they would have to pay the costs, and couldn't commit Uptown to paying any money without Uptown's permission.

If there is any lawsuit, or any other settlement of disputes that results in a payment to either the composer or the publisher, then the publisher and composer are to split the proceeds remaining after any expenses are deducted. As with any other money that the songwriter would otherwise be entitled to under the agreement, if there are any advances to be recouped, the publisher can apply the songwriter's share of any lawsuit or settlement proceeds to those advances.

> *If there is any recovery made by either party hereto as a result of any litigation with respect to the Composition, then after deduction of the reasonable expenses of litigation, including without limitation reasonable outside attorney's fees and court costs, fifty percent (50%) of such net proceeds remaining shall be paid to Publisher for its own account, and fifty percent (50%) thereof shall be paid to or retained by Composer. Publisher, whenever, in its opinion, its right, title or interest to the Composition is questioned or there is a breach of any of the covenants or warranties contained herein, may withhold any and all royalties that may be or become due to Composer hereunder in an amount reasonably related to the risk of such claim plus Publisher's estimated attorney's fees in connection therewith until such question shall have been settled or such breach repaired, and may apply such royalties to the repayment of all sums due Publisher hereunder. Upon the final adjudication or settlement of each and every claim hereunder, all monies withheld shall be disbursed in accordance with the rights of the parties as provided herein.*

You should note that the publisher can suspend royalties in order to build a fund from which to pay any amounts that might come due. An alternative provision would the songwriter to post such a bond in lieu of having royalties suspended.

For instance, the author was recently involved in a lawsuit against several songwriters. The plaintiff sent the songwriters, the publisher, and a number of other parties a letter claiming an interest in several of the songwriters' compositions. The songwriters refused to acknowledge the claim, and the plaintiff filed suit, claiming damages of several million dollars. Once the publisher decided that the plaintiff was not going away, it began to suspend the songwriters' income, in order to have enough money set aside to cover mounting attorney's fees and any other losses it might suffer. The contract contained a clause that allowed the songwriter to post a bond in order to have those royalties released. Be aware, however, that a bond almost always requires an upfront premium of approximately 10% of the face value, plus collateral in the amount of the face value. Furthermore, although the bond will pay out if the suit is lost, that money has to be paid back. Therefore, as much as the songwriter may want royalties released, he or she may have to pass on the bond because of the expense.

Where a song has more than one author, the agreement will bind all of them:

> *Composer includes all authors and composers of the Composition. If there shall be more than one, the covenants herein shall be joint and several on the part of such authors and composers and the royalties specified herein shall be divided between them as indicated hereunder.*

For instance, where Fred, Joe and Bob co-wrote a song, all of the terms of this agreement apply to all of them, and they are expected to split the income from the publisher in whatever proportion that they contributed to the authorship of the song. Another important point to note is that each individual songwriter carries full liability for any problems. Assume, for instance, that Fred, Joe, Bob and Uptown settle a suit filed by another songwriter for copyright infringement and Uptown pays the settlement in the amount of $50,000. If Joe and Bob have squandered all of their income on cars and women, Uptown can demand full reimbursement from Fred (who invested all of his in money markets), even though he is only partially responsible for the authorship of the song. Fred can, of course, demand that Joe and Bob reimburse him for their share of the cost, but if Joe and Bob are broke, Fred is not likely to get his money back. Keep in mind, too, that songwriter percentages are frequently uneven. Therefore, if Bob wrote all lyrics and claimed 50% ownership, Joe wrote most of the music and claimed 45% ownership and Fred contributed a "bridge" in the middle for an ownership of 5%, then in this situation, Fred could be held responsible for 100% of the costs when he only received 5% of the income.

Conclusion

Without a doubt, non-exclusive songwriter agreements are the most common songwriter arrangements, so it's important to understand how they are used. It is imperative for a publisher to have a songwriter agreement in place for every song that the publisher owns. Outside of some other grant of rights (which is usually more vague and may be difficult to stand on), if a songwriter agreement is not in place, then the publisher cannot be assured that it owns the song. Without that assurance, the publisher cannot guarantee the record label that a grant of rights to reproduce and distribute is valid.

In the next chapter, we'll explore another arrangement between a publisher and songwriter, the Exclusive Songwriter Agreement. As you will see, even if there is an exclusive arrangement, it is still important to maintain separate Non-Exclusive Songwriter Agreements for every song in the catalog. This will help ensure that every individual song is protected, even if there is ever a problem with the employment arrangement that the Exclusive Songwriter Agreement creates.

Form
Non-exclusive Songwriter Agreement

Agreement made on _____, 20__, by and between _____ Publishing Company (hereinafter referred to as "Publisher") and John J. Songwriter (hereinafter referred to as "Composer"), in connection with the composition entitled "_____" written solely by the Composer (hereinafter referred to as the "Composition").

1. GRANT OF RIGHTS

Composer assigns to Publisher, in perpetuity, all of his worldwide rights in the Composition, including without limitation, the title, words, and music thereof: all copyrights with respect thereto and the right to secure any extensions and renewals in the same and in any arrangements and adaptations thereof: and all other rights, which now or hereafter may exist at law or by agreement relating thereto. Composer irrevocably appoints Publisher, or any of its officers, his attorney, empowered to sign any instruments which Publisher may deem necessary to vest itself, its successors, assigns, and licensees, and of the rights referred to herein. Publisher may for the term of this Agreement use throughout the world Composer's name and likeness in connection with the use of the Composition, including without limitation printed versions thereof, and in connection with publicity and advertising concerning Publisher. Publisher may make arrangements, adaptations, translations and dramatizations of the Composition, and add new lyrics in a language other than English to the music of the Composition. Publisher shall collect all income earned by the Composition.

2. COMPENSATION

a. Publisher shall pay Composer fifty percent (50%) of all net sums actually received in the United States by Publisher and all allocable to the Composition for mechanical rights, print rights, synchronization rights and for any other use or exploitation of the Composition anywhere in the world: provided, however, Composer shall collect his public performance royalties throughout the world directly from his own affiliated performing rights society and shall have no claim whatsoever against Publisher for the "publisher's share" (as such term is commonly understood in the worldwide music industry) of any royalties received by Publisher from any performing rights society.

b.   Publisher shall render royalty statements to Composer at least twice per year, but only for accounting periods in which royalties accrue. Statements will be accompanied by appropriate payments, if any. A Certified Public Accountant or attorney on Composer's behalf may examine the books of Publisher pertaining to the Composition during Publisher's usual business hours and upon thirty (30) days prior notice. Said books relating to activities and receipts during any accounting period may be examined as aforesaid only once and only during the two (2) year period following issuance of the statement for said accounting period. The supporting documents for any statement may be examined only once by Composer. If Composer does not institute a lawsuit within one (1) year of conducting an audit, then Composer shall forever be barred from making a claim as to the audited statement.

3.   WARRANTIES AND REPRESENTATIONS

a.   Composer warrants that the Composition is an original work, created solely by Composer, and will not infringe any copyright or violate or interfere with any interest, whether contractual, statutory, or otherwise, of any third party. Composer shall indemnify Publisher, its assigns, licensees and employees from any and all liability or claims including reasonable outside attorneys fees and court costs arising out of or related to any claim inconsistent with any warranty or representation, express or implied, made by Composer herein.

b.   Publisher, at its discretion, may employ attorneys and institute or defend any claim or action either in Composer's name, and take any necessary proper steps to protect the right, title and interest of Publisher in and to the Composition and in that connection to settle, compromise or in any other manner dispose of any such claim, action or judgment that may be rendered. Notwithstanding the foregoing, Composer may, through legal counsel of Composer's choice, assume control of any dispute. Publisher will not incur any costs payable by Composer without Composer's consent.

c.   If there is any recovery made by either party hereto as a result of any litigation with respect to the Composition, then after deduction of the reasonable expenses of litigation, including without limitation reasonable outside attorney's fees and court costs, fifty percent (50%) of such net proceeds remaining shall be paid to Publisher for its own account, and fifty percent (50%) thereof shall be paid to or retained by Composer. Publisher, whenever, in its opinion, its right, title or interest to the Composition is questioned or there is a breach of any of the covenants or warranties contained herein, may withhold any and all royalties that may be or become due to Composer hereunder in an amount reasonably related to the risk of such claim plus Publisher's estimated attorney's fees in connection therewith until such question shall have been settled or such breach repaired, and may apply such royalties to the repayment of all sums due Publisher hereunder. Upon the final adjudication or settlement of each and every claim hereunder, all monies withheld shall be disbursed in accordance with the rights of the parties as provided herein.

4. AUTHORSHIP AND OWNERSHIP

   a. Composer includes all authors and composers of the Composition. If there shall be more than one, the covenants herein shall be joint and several on the part of such authors and composers and the royalties specified herein shall be divided between them as indicated hereunder.

   b. The following are all authors of the Composition, along with the percentage of such authorship:

   c. The following are all publishers of the Composition, along with each publisher's percentage:

6. MISCELLANEOUS

This agreement may be executed by all authors in several counterparts. Publisher may assign any of its rights or obligations hereunder to any other party without prior consent of Composer. All notices, statements and payments given hereunder shall be sent to the parties at the addresses indicated herein, or to such other address as any party may designate by written notice to the other party(ies). Notices shall be in writing and shall be delivered personally or to any officer if the party is a corporation, or by certified or registered mail. This agreement sets forth the entire understanding of the parties and cannot be amended, terminated or rescinded except by an instrument signed by all parties hereto. If any part hereof shall be invalid or unenforceable it shall not effect the validity of the remainder of this agreement. This agreement shall be governed by and construed in accordance with the laws of the State of _____ applicable to agreements made and performed entirely therein.

Chapter 3

The Exclusive Songwriter:
So What's the Difference?

Many people are born songwriters, but have no desire to be recording artists. Although record label-publishers frequently sign their artists as exclusive songwriters, or may contract with non-artist songwriters on a song-by-song basis, the exclusive songwriter arrangement is most common for songwriters who are not artists.

An Exclusive Songwriter Agreement is similar in many respects to the Non-Exclusive Songwriter Agreement. Obviously, the main difference is in the exclusive rights to the writer's services. A company that hires a songwriter on an exclusive basis will own the rights to all songs written by the songwriter during the term of the contract. In return, this arrangement will generally involve some type of regular payments.

As you will see, some of the terms in the Exclusive Songwriter Agreement are very similar to the Non-Exclusive Agreement. We have included them in this segment so you can be aware of all of the provisions that would be contained in such an agreement, and so you can see examples of how the wording might be different. However, because the similar terms have been fully discussed above, the explanations in this section are abbreviated.

A. Engagement

The publisher essentially hires the songwriter as a staff member:

Publisher hereby employs Writer to render Writer's services as a songwriter and composer and otherwise as may hereinafter be set forth. Writer hereby accepts such employment and agrees to render such services exclusively for Publisher during the term hereof, upon the terms and conditions set forth herein.

B. Term

Similar to the Recording Artist Agreement, the contract is usually set up with an initial period and then a few options, exercisable at the company's election.

> *The initial term of this Agreement shall commence as of the date of execution and shall continue for an initial term of two (2) years. Writer hereby grants to Publisher two (2) separate and irrevocable options, each to renew this Agreement for a one (1) year term, such renewal terms to run consecutively beginning at the expiration of the initial term hereof, all upon the same terms and conditions as are applicable to the initial term except as otherwise provided herein. Each option shall be exercised only by written notice to be sent by Publisher to Writer not less than ten (10) days prior to the commencement of the renewal term for which the option is exercised.*

Here, the songwriter can expect to render his or her services as a songwriter for at least two years. If the publisher decides that the songwriter is an asset to the company, then the publisher can decide to extend the term. Consider our hypothetical writers Fred and Bob. Within the first year, Fred has written 24 songs, seven of which were placed with a recording artist and three of which made the top ten on the charts. Bob, on the other hand, wrote 30 songs, none of which were even placed. The publisher, Uptown Music Co., will likely extend Fred's contract, but may allow Bob's to lapse after the second year.

Biz Note: As a general rule, when an exclusive songwriter agreement is signed as part of a record deal negotiation, the exclusive songwriter agreement should terminate at the same time the record deal terminates.

C. Grant of Rights

When the songwriter signs on with the publisher, the songwriter can expect to give up all rights in his or her compositions.

> *Writer hereby irrevocably and absolutely assigns, conveys and grants to Publisher, its successors and assigns (a) all rights and interests of*

every kind, nature and description in and to all original musical com-
positions and all original arrangements of musical compositions in the
public domain which have heretofore been written, composed or created
by Writer, in whole or in part, alone or in collaboration with others,
including but not limited to the titles, lyrics and music thereof and all
world-wide copyrights and renewals and extensions thereof under any
present or future laws throughout the world, to the extent any of the
foregoing shall not heretofore have been conveyed by Writer to an unre-
lated third party; and (b) all rights and interests of every kind, nature
and description in and to the results and proceeds of Writer's services
hereunder, including but not limited to the titles, lyrics and music of all
original musical compositions and of all original arrangements of
musical compositions in the public domain and all world-wide copy-
rights and renewals and extensions thereof under any present or future
laws throughout the world, which shall be written, composed or created
by Writer during the term hereof, in whole or in part, alone or in col-
laboration with others; and (c) all rights and interests of every kind,
nature and description in and to all original musical compositions and
all original arrangements of musical compositions in the public domain
which are now directly or indirectly owned or controlled by Writer, in
whole or in part, alone or with others, or the direct or indirect owner-
ship or control of which shall be acquired by Writer during the term
hereof, in whole or in part, alone or with others, as the employer or
transferee of the writers or composers thereof or otherwise, including
the titles, lyrics and music thereof and all world-wide copyrights and
renewals and extensions thereof under any present or future laws
throughout the world; all of which musical compositions, arrange-
ments, rights and interests Writer hereby warrants and represents are
and shall at all times be Publisher's exclusive property as the sole owner
thereof, free from any adverse claims or rights therein by any other
party (all such musical compositions and arrangements hereinafter
being referred to as "Compositions.")

Without limiting the generality of the foregoing, Writer acknowl-
edges that the rights and interests hereinabove set forth include Writer's
irrevocable grant to Publisher, its successors and assigns, of the sole and
exclusive right, license, privilege and authority throughout the entire
world with respect to all Compositions, whether now in existence or
whether created during the term hereof, as follows:

a. *To perform and license others to perform the Compositions publicly or privately, for profit or otherwise, by means of public or private performance, radio broadcast, television, or any and all other means of media, whether now known or hereafter conceived or developed.*

b. *To substitute a new title or titles for the Compositions or any of them and to make any arrangement, adaptation, translation, dramatization or transposition of any or all of the Compositions or of the titles, lyrics or music thereof, in whole or in part, and in connection with any other musical, literary or dramatic material, and to add new lyrics to the music of any Compositions or new music to the lyrics of any Compositions, all as Publisher may deem necessary or desirable in its best business judgment.*

c. *To secure copyright registration and protection of the Compositions in Publisher's name or otherwise, as Publisher may desire, at Publisher's own cost and expense, and at Publisher's election, including any and all renewals and extensions of copyright under any present or future laws throughout the world, and to have and to hold said copyrights, renewals and extensions and all rights existing thereunder, for and during the full term of all said copyrights and all renewals and extensions and all rights existing thereunder, for and during the full term of all said copyrights and all renewals and extensions thereof.*

d. *To make or cause to be made, and to license others to make, master records, transcriptions, soundtracks, pressings and any other mechanical, electrical or other reproductions of the Compositions, in whole or in part, in such form or manner and as frequently as Publisher shall determine, including the right to synchronize the Compositions with sound motion pictures and to use, manufacture, advertise, license or sell such reproductions for any and all purposes, including, without limitation private and public performances, radio broadcast, television, sound motion pictures, wired radio, phonograph records and any and all other means or devices, whether now known or hereafter conceived or developed.*

e. *To print, publish and sell, and to license others to print, publish and sell, sheet music, orchestrations, arrangements and other editions of the Compositions in all forms, including, without limitation, the inclusion of any or all of the Compositions in song folios, compilations, song books, mixed folios, personality folios and lyric magazines with or without music.*

f.   *Any and all other rights now or hereafter existing in all Compositions under and by virtue of any common law rights and all copyrights and renewals and extensions thereof including so-called small performance rights. Writer grants to Publisher, without any compensation other than as specified herein, the perpetual right to use and publish and to permit others to use and publish Writer's name (including any professional name heretofore or hereafter adopted by Writer), Writer's photograph or other likeness, or any reproduction or simulation thereof, and biographical material concerning Writer, and the titles of any and all of the Compositions, in connection with the printing, sale, advertising, performance, distribution and other exploitation of the Compositions, and for any other purpose related to the business of Publisher, its affiliated and related companies, or to refrain therefrom. This right shall be exclusive during the term hereof and nonexclusive thereafter. Writer shall not authorize or permit the use of Writer's name or likeness, or any reproduction or simulation thereof, or biographical material concerning Writer, for or in connection with any musical compositions, other than by or for Publisher. Writer grants Publisher the right to refer to Writer as Publisher's "Exclusive Songwriter and Composer" or to use any other similar and appropriate appellation, during the term hereof.*

This is a whole lot of legalese for "all rights to everything the Composer has written to date or will write until the contract ends." This provision transfers all rights that go along with a composition to the publisher, whether the song was written prior to execution of the contract or while the contract is in effect. If the songwriter has already transferred the rights in the song to a third party, then that song is excluded. Therefore, if Fred, prior to signing the deal with Uptown, had written ten songs, then those ten songs would belong to Uptown, as well as everything Fred created during the contract term. However, if Fred wrote one of those ten songs, "Old Faithful," as a tribute to his best friend's dog, then transferred all rights in the song to the friend for his birthday, that song would not go to Uptown. If Fred co-wrote another of the ten songs, "Down Trodd'n," with Steve, then Fred's share would go to the publisher and Steve's share would remain unaffected.

You should note that these rights do not expire with the contract. The assignment of rights is permanent, unless the contract allows a reversion, as discussed below. The publisher also has the permanent right to use the songwriter's name and likeness (photograph, biographical information, etc.), although the right becomes non-exclusive when the contract expires.

D. Services

The heart of the agreement is the exclusive claim to the songwriter's services:

> *During the term of this Agreement, Writer shall not write or compose, or furnish or convey, any musical compositions, titles, lyrics or music, or any rights or interests therein, nor participate in any manner with regard to same, for or to any party other than Publisher, nor permit the use of his name or likeness as the writer or co-writer of any musical composition by any party other than Publisher.*

When the songwriter signs the agreement, he or she cannot write songs for any other publisher. Not even one song—or part of a song. Note, too, that the songwriter cannot let any other publisher use his or her name or photograph in connection with songwriting. However, if the songwriter had a previous deal with another publisher, the songwriter would want to make sure that publisher was accommodated. For instance, if Bob, before signing with Uptown, had an exclusive deal with Suburban Publishing, Bob would have to make sure that this contract allowed Suburban the right to use his name in connection with the songs that he wrote while with them. If Bob didn't make sure that this exception was included, then he would be in breach of his contract with Suburban, since their agreement would have included the perpetual right to use his name and likeness in connection with their compositions.

E. Warranties

As with many other contracts, the songwriter has to make certain representations before the publisher will agree to engage him or her.

> *Writer hereby warrants, represents, covenants and agrees as follows: Writer has the full right, power and authority to enter into and perform this Agreement and to grant to and vest in Publisher all rights herein set forth, free and clear of any and all claims, rights and obligations whatsoever; all of the Compositions and all other results and proceeds of the*

services of Writer hereunder, including all of the titles, lyrics and music of the Compositions and each and every part thereof, delivered and to be delivered by Writer hereunder are and shall be new and original and capable of copyright protection throughout the entire world; no Composition shall, either in whole or in part, be an imitation or copy of, or infringe upon, any other material, or violate or infringe upon any common law or statutory rights of any party including, without limitation, contractual rights, copyrights and rights of privacy; and Writer has not sold, assigned, leased, licensed or in any other way disposed of or encumbered any Composition, in whole or in part, or any rights herein granted to Publisher, nor shall Writer sell, assign, lease, license or in any other way dispose of or encumber any of the Compositions, in whole or in part, or any of said rights, except under the terms and conditions hereof.

It isn't enough for Fred to hand over all rights to the publisher—he has to confirm that those rights are worth something. If the songs have owners that Fred hasn't mentioned, writers Fred hasn't credited, or in some other way is going to create a lawsuit for the publisher, then Uptown might have decided not to sign the contract, or at least to lower the price. These representations give the publisher something to point to if something goes wrong.

F. Power of Attorney

The songwriter has to allow the publisher to complete whatever paperwork is necessary to confirm its ownership.

Writer hereby irrevocably constitutes, authorizes, empowers and appoints Publisher or any of its officers Writer's true and lawful attorney (with full power of substitution and delegation), in Writer's name, and in Writer's place and stead, or in Publisher's name, to take and do such action, and to make, sign, execute, acknowledge and deliver any and all instruments or documents, which Publisher from time to time may deem desirable or necessary to vest in Publisher, its successors and assigns, all of the rights or interests granted by Writer hereunder, including, without limitation, such documents as Publisher shall deem desirable or necessary to secure to Publisher, its successors and assigns, the worldwide copyrights for all Compositions for the entire term of copyright and for any and all renewals and extensions under any present or future laws throughout the world.

Notwithstanding the foregoing, Writer acknowledges that he (or she) is Publisher's employee for hire that all Compositions are and shall be works made for hire and that Publisher is accordingly the author of all Compositions for all purposes under United States Copyright Law.

This clause grants the publisher power of attorney to sign, on behalf of the songwriter, whatever documents are necessary to give the publisher ownership of the compositions. As a practical matter, most publishers will at least attempt to get the songwriter's signature before using this power of attorney.

You should also note that this agreement contains a "work for hire" provision. Since the songwriter is an employee for the publisher, the compositions are considered to be "authored" by the publisher. Under a work for hire arrangement, the songwriter has no rights in the compositions in the first place.

G. Compensation

As we discussed above, there are several ways that a publisher may pay royalties. The non-exclusive agreement promised royalties in general terms: 50% of everything the publisher makes after deducting expenses. Here is an example of a more specific provision:

Provided that Writer shall duly perform the terms, covenants and conditions of this Agreement, Publisher shall pay Writer, for the services to be rendered by Writer hereunder and for the rights acquired and to be acquired by Publisher hereunder, the following compensation based on the Compositions:

a. *Ten cents ($.10) per copy for each copy of sheet music in standard piano/vocal notation and each dance orchestration printed, published and sold in the United States and Canada by Publisher or its licensees, for which payment shall have been received by Publisher, after deduction of returns.*

b. *Ten percent (10%) of the wholesale selling price of each printed copy of each other arrangement and edition printed, published and sold in the United States and Canada by Publisher or its licensees, for which payment shall have been received by Publisher, after deduction of returns, except that in the event that any Compositions shall be used or caused to be used, in whole or in part, in conjunction with one or more other musical compositions in a folio, compilation, song book or other publication, Writer shall be entitled to receive that proportion of the foregoing royalty which the number of Compositions contained therein shall bear to the total number of musical compositions therein.*

c.   *Fifty percent (50%) of any and all net sums actually received (less any costs for collection) by Publisher in the United States from the exploitation in the United States and Canada by licensees of mechanical rights, electrical transcription and reproduction rights, motion picture and television synchronization rights, dramatization rights and all other rights therein (except print rights, which are covered in (a) and (b) above, and public performance rights, which are covered in (d) below), whether or not such licensees are affiliated with, owned in whole or in part by, or controlled by Publisher.*

d.   *Writer shall receive his public performance royalties throughout the world directly from the performing rights society with which he is affiliated, and shall have no claim whatsoever against Publisher for any royalties received by Publisher from any performing rights society which makes payment directly (or indirectly other than through Publisher) to writers, authors and composers. If, however, Publisher shall collect both the Writer's and Publisher's share of performance income directly and such income shall not be collected by Writer's public performance society, Publisher shall pay to Writer fifty percent (50%) of all such net sums which are received by Publisher in the United States from the exploitation of such rights in the Compositions, throughout the world.*

e.   *Fifty percent (50%) of any and all net sums, after deduction of foreign taxes, actually received (less any costs for collection) by Publisher in the United States from the exploitation of the Compositions in countries outside of the United States and Canada (other than public performance royalties, which are covered in (d) above), whether from collection agents, licensees, subpublishers or others, and whether or not same are affiliated with, owned in whole or in part by, or controlled by Publisher.*

f.   *Publisher shall not be required to pay any royalties on professional or complimentary printed copies or records or on printed copies or records which are distributed gratuitously to performing artists, orchestra leaders and disc jockeys or for advertising, promotional or exploitation purposes. Furthermore, no royalties shall be payable to Writer on consigned copies unless paid for, and not until such time as an accounting therefor can properly be made.*

g. *Royalties as hereinabove specified shall be payable solely to Writer in instances where Writer is the sole author of a Composition, including the lyrics and music thereof. However, in the event that one or more other songwriters are authors together with Writer of any Composition (including songwriters employed by Publisher to add, change or translate the lyrics or to revise or change the music), the foregoing royalties shall be divided equally among Writer and the other songwriters unless another division of royalties shall be agreed upon in writing between the parties concerned and timely written notice of such division is submitted to Publisher prior to payment.*

h. *Except as herein expressly provided, no other royalties or monies shall be paid to Writer.*

i. *Writer agrees and acknowledges that Publisher shall have the right to withhold from the royalties payable to Writer hereunder such amount, if any, as may be required under the provisions of all applicable Federal, State and other tax laws and regulations, and Writer agrees to execute such forms and other documents as may be required in connection therewith.*

j. *In no event shall Writer be entitled to share in any advance payments, guarantee payments or minimum royalty payments which Publisher shall receive in connection with any subpublishing agreement, collection agreement, licensing agreement or other agreement covering the Compositions or any of them.*

This provision provides a flat rate for sheet music ($0.10 each), a reduced percentage of non-standard printed music (10%), half of the mechanical royalties (after costs) and half of the foreign royalties (after costs). As with the non-exclusive agreement, the songwriter collects performance royalties directly from BMI, ASCAP or SESAC.

H. Accounting

As with any other music industry agreement, the publisher must account to the writer for all monies that the publisher makes in connection with the songwriter's compositions.

> *Publisher shall compute the royalties earned by Writer pursuant to this Agreement and pursuant to any other agreement between Writer and Publisher or its affiliates, whether now in existence or entered into at any time subsequent hereto, on or before March 31st for the semiannual period ending the preceding December 31st and on or before September 30th for the semiannual period ending the preceding June 30th, and shall thereupon submit to Writer the royalty statement for each such period together with the net amount of royalties, if any, which shall be payable after deducting any and all unrecouped advances and chargeable costs under this Agreement or any such other agreement. Each statement submitted by Publisher to Writer shall be binding upon Writer and not subject to any objection by Writer for any reason unless specific written objection, stating the basis thereof, is sent by Writer to Publisher within one (1) year after the date said statement is submitted. Writer or a certified public accountant in Writer's behalf may, at Writer's expense, at reasonable intervals (but not more frequent than once each year), examine Publisher's books insofar as same concern Writer, during Publisher's usual business hours and upon reasonable notice, for the purpose of verifying the accuracy of any statement submitted to Writer hereunder. Publisher's books relating to activities during any accounting period may only be examined as aforesaid during the one (1) year period following service by Publisher of the statement for said accounting period.*

This provision provides for accountings twice a year, along with payment of any royalties remaining after advances to the songwriter are deducted. Like the non-exclusive agreement, the songwriter that objects to a statement must provide written notice within the time provided, which is one year in this provision. The songwriter's C.P.A. may audit the publisher, as long as the audit is within one year of the time the statement is issued, and so long as audits are at least a year apart.

I. Collaboration

Many exclusive publishing agreements require co-writers to assign their publishing to the publisher, although only for the composition at issue.

> *Whenever Writer shall collaborate with any other person in the creation of a Composition, the Composition shall be subject to the terms and conditions of this Agreement, and Writer warrants, represents and agrees that prior to such collaboration Writer shall advise such other person of this exclusive Agreement and shall further advise such other person that all Compositions so created must be published and owned by Publisher. In the event of any such collaboration, Writer shall notify Publisher of the nature and extent of such other person's contribution to the Composition, and Writer shall cause such other person to execute a separate songwriter's agreement with Publisher covering the Composition, which agreement shall set forth the division of the songwriter's royalties between Writer and such other person, and Publisher shall make payment accordingly.*

This is not as much of an issue if the co-writer does not have an exclusive publisher. However, if the co-writer has a contractual relationship with a publisher (or a big enough name to insist on keeping his or her own publishing), then this must be addressed PRIOR to collaborating.

Biz note: This is a fairly hard line approach, and most publishers will allow the songwriters with whom the exclusive songwriter is collaborating to keep their publishing. However, as discussed below, if the exclusive songwriter has a quota to maintain during the term of the contract, any portion of a song not written by the exclusive songwriter does not count toward the quota unless it is published by the publisher.

J. Individual Songwriter Agreements

Publisher's generally have a "catalog" of works, meaning that they own a substantial number of compositions. These compositions are a commodity that are licensed to numerous entities, and bought and traded with other publishers on a fairly regular basis. In order to make it easier for the publisher to work with the compositions on an individual basis, the publisher should have the composer sign a separate agreement for each song, in addition to the exclusive songwriter agreement. The separate agreement is essentially the non-exclusive agreement set forth in chapter 2.

> *If Publisher so desires, Publisher may request Writer to execute a separate agreement in Publisher's customary form with respect to each Composition hereunder. Upon such request, Writer shall promptly execute and deliver such separate agreement, and upon Writer's failure to do so, Publisher shall have the right, pursuant to the terms and conditions hereof, to execute such separate agreement in behalf of Writer. Such separate agreement shall supplement and not supersede this Agreement. In the event of any conflict between the provisions of such separate agreement and this Agreement, the provisions of this Agreement shall govern. The failure of either of the parties hereto to execute such separate agreement, whether such execution is requested by Publisher or not, shall not affect the rights of each of the parties hereunder, including but not limited to the rights of Publisher to all of the Compositions written, composed or acquired by Writer during the term hereof.*

K. Duties and Responsibilities

Both the songwriter and the publisher will have some specific responsibilities under the agreement. The songwriter must deliver work tapes and lyric sheets as soon as each composition is completed. The publisher will then use its best efforts to promote each song. However, the publisher has the discretion to decide which songs are the most marketable and to focus its efforts accordingly, even if publisher elects not to promote any of the songs at all.

> *a.   Writer shall perform his or her required services hereunder conscientiously, and solely and exclusively for and as requested by Publisher. Writer shall duly comply with all requirements and requests made by Publisher in connection with its business as set forth herein. Writer shall deliver a manuscript copy or tape copy of each Composition immediately upon the completion or acquisition of such Composition. Publisher shall use its reasonable efforts in its best business judgment to exploit all Compositions hereunder, but Publisher's failure to exploit any or all of said Compositions shall not be deemed a breach hereof. Publisher at its sole discretion shall reasonably make studio facilities available for Writer so that Writer, subject to the supervision and control of Publisher, may*

produce demonstration records of the Compositions, and Writer shall have the right to perform at such recording sessions. Publisher shall also have the right to produce demonstration records hereunder. Writer shall not incur any liability for which Publisher shall be responsible in connection with any demonstration record session without having obtained Publisher's prior written approval as to the nature, extent and limit of such liability. In no event shall Writer incur any expense whatsoever on behalf of Publisher without having obtained prior written authorization from Publisher. Writer shall not be entitled to any compensation (except for such compensation as is otherwise provided for herein) with respect to services rendered in connection with any such demonstration record sessions. Publisher shall advance the costs for the production of demonstration records, subject to the foregoing, and one-half (1/2) of such costs shall be deemed additional advances to Writer hereunder and shall be recouped by Publisher from royalties payable to Writer by Publisher under this Agreement or any other agreement between Writer and Publisher or its affiliates. All recordings and reproductions made at demonstration record sessions hereunder shall become the sole and exclusive property of Publisher, free of any claims whatsoever by Writer or any person deriving any rights from Writer.

One tool that the publisher will use to promote a song is a demo. Therefore, this provision addresses the creation of demo recordings. The publisher can make arrangements to produce demos whenever it feels a demo would be useful, and the publisher will front the costs for the demo. However, the writer may not obligate the publisher to pay the cost of demo recordings without the publisher's prior approval. Although the publisher is fronting the costs, one half of those costs must be repaid by the writer through his or her royalties. Of course, the publisher will own all demos.

Many exclusive songwriter agreements have a minimum requirement that a composer must adhere to. Although this may seem impractical from a creative standpoint (many artists believe that inspiration doesn't strike on a timetable) the publisher wants to ensure that their employee is actually earning the salary he or she is being paid.

   b.   Writer agrees to produce a minimum of twenty-four (24) complete songs per year, or two (2) complete Compositions per month. The percentage of any Composition hereunder written by any composer

> *other than Writer shall not be applied toward Writer's obligations under this agreement. No Composition will be credited to Writer's obligations until a lyric sheet, work tape, and any documents required by Publisher for such Composition are delivered to Publisher.*

The provision also addresses how the minimum song requirement, two per month in this example, is affected when the songwriter collaborates with another composer. If Fred decides to collaborate with his friend Larry, and Larry's publishing belongs to another publisher, then Fred only gets credit for one half of a song (or whatever portion Fred ends up writing) and must write more music in order to comply with his minimum commitment. You should also note that the song is not considered to be "produced" until a lyric sheet, work tape and other documents, such as individual songwriter agreements as discussed below, are actually delivered to the publisher.

Furthermore, a songwriter must understand that just any old song won't do. The composition must be "commercially viable."

> c.   *Writer agrees that each Composition composed hereunder shall be subject to Publisher's approval as "Commercially Viable." As used herein, Compositions shall be deemed "Commercially Viable" if they are of a style and quality consistent with Writer's previous compositions and if Publisher believes, in good faith, that the subject Composition realistically can be marketed to the public.*

To be commercially viable, the song must be at least as good as the songwriter's prior works and must be good enough to be marketed to the public. There are several circumstances where this is important. For instance, if Fred has a family emergency that occupies most of a month, he may be tempted to throw something together and turn it in to satisfy his writing requirement. This provision would prevent him from doing that unless the end result was marketable. Naturally there is no formula for this determination, but the requirement will, at the very least, prevent a songwriter from deliberately delivering substandard materials.

The songwriter will be required to assist in promoting the compositions by making public appearances and sitting for photographs and the like, as reasonably necessary.

> d.   *Writer shall, from time to time, at Publisher's reasonable request, and whenever same will not unreasonably interfere with prior*

professional engagements of Writer, appear for photography, art-
work and other similar purposes under the direction of Publisher
or its duly authorized agent, appear for interviews and other pro-
motional purposes, and confer and consult with Publisher or its
duly authorized agent, appear for interviews and other promo-
tional purposes, and confer and consult with Publisher regarding
Writer's services hereunder. Writer shall also cooperate with
Publisher in promoting, publicizing and exploiting the
Compositions and for any other purpose related to the business of
Publisher. Writer shall not be entitled to any compensation (other
than applicable union scale if appropriate) for rendering such
services, but shall be entitled to reasonable transportation and liv-
ing expenses if such expenses must be incurred in order to render
such services.

L. Protecting the Compositions

Similar to the Non-exclusive Agreement, the publisher may sue to protect the composition, settle the claims or defend any claims against the composition. Any proceeds are split between the parties, after the costs are deducted.

Publisher shall have the exclusive right to take such action as it
deems necessary, either in Writer's name or in its own name or in both
names, against any party to protect all rights and interests acquired by
Publisher hereunder. Writer shall, cooperate fully with Publisher in any
controversy which may arise or litigation which may be brought con-
cerning Publisher's rights and interests acquired hereunder. Publisher
shall have the right, in its discretion, to employ attorneys and to insti-
tute or defend against any claim, action or proceeding, whether for
infringement of copyright or otherwise, and to take any other necessary
steps to protect the right, title and interest of Publisher in and to each
Composition and, in connection therewith, to settle, compromise or in
any other manner dispose of any such claim, action or proceeding and
to satisfy or collect on any judgment which may be rendered. If
Publisher shall recover on a judgment or as a result of a settlement with
respect to any claim, action or proceeding for copyright infringement
initiated by Publisher, all of Publisher's expenses in connection there-
with, including, without limitation, attorney's fees and other costs, shall
first be deducted, and fifty percent (50%) of the net proceeds shall be
credited to Writer's account.

M. Indemnity

The publisher will also require a promise from the songwriter to repay the publisher for expenses incurred if any problems arise.

> *Writer hereby indemnifies, saves and holds Publisher, its successors and assigns, harmless from any and all liability, claims, demands, loss and damage (including counsel fees and court costs) arising out of or connected with any claim or action by a third party which is inconsistent with any of the warranties, representations or agreements made by Writer in this Agreement, and Writer shall reimburse Publisher, on demand, for any loss, cost, expense or damage to which said indemnity applies. Publisher shall give Writer prompt written notice of any claim or action covered by said indemnity, and Writer shall have the right, at Writer's expense, to participate in the defense of any such claim or action with counsel of Writer's choice. Pending the disposition of any such claim or action, Publisher shall have the right to withhold payment of such portion of any monies which may be payable by Publisher to Writer under this Agreement or under any other agreement between Writer and Publisher or its affiliates as shall be reasonably related to the amount of the claim and estimated counsel fees and costs. If Publisher shall settle or compromise any such claim or action, the foregoing indemnity shall cover only that portion (if any) of the settlement or compromise which shall have been approved in writing by Writer, and Writer hereby agrees not unreasonably to withhold any such approval. Notwithstanding the foregoing, if Writer shall withhold approval of any settlement or compromise which Publisher is willing to make upon advice of counsel and in its best business judgment, Writer shall thereupon deliver to Publisher an indemnity or surety bond, in form satisfactory to Publisher, which shall cover the amount of the claim and estimated counsel fees and costs, and if Writer shall fail to deliver such bond within ten (10) business days, Writer shall be deemed to have approved of said settlement or compromise.*

This example contains a provision that allows the songwriter to refuse a settlement offer, if he or she is willing to post a bond that will cover all costs, including payments to the plaintiffs if the case is ultimately lost.

N. Scheduled Payments

Because an exclusive songwriter is an employee, he or she is usually paid a salary. The salary, however, is recoupable from any royalties accrued.

> *Conditioned upon, and in consideration of, the full and faithful performance by Writer of all of the terms and provisions hereof, Publisher shall pay to Writer _____ on the first day of each month during the term hereof, all of which payments shall be recoupable by Publisher from any and all royalties payable to Writer under this or any other agreement between Writer and Publisher and from any and all monies payable to Writer's designee under the Participation Agreement described below*

The record company comes back into play here. This provision allows the songwriter's record company to recoup the publishing advances. This is called "cross collateralization." So, when Fred signs with Uptown Music, the publishing affiliate of Livin' Large Records, whatever money Uptown gives him as an advance can be recovered from both his songwriting royalties *and* his artist royalties from Livin' Large Records, assuming there are any royalties left after Livin' Large has recouped all of its recording costs (which is not likely). This also works in the reverse: if Livin' Large does not recoup all recording costs from the artist's royalties, it can recoup from the songwriter royalties.

> *It is understood and acknowledged that any and all charges or advances against royalties under this agreement which are not recouped by Publisher may be recouped by Publisher's record company affiliate or its assignee from any and all royalties earned by Writer under the aforementioned recording contract or its successor or replacement agreement, and that any and all charges or advances against royalties under said recording contract or its successor or replacement agreement which are not recouped by said record company or its assignee may be recouped by Publisher from any and all royalties earned by Writer hereunder.*

Biz note: This is also a hard line position, and it is very rare for a record company/publisher to insist on cross-collateralization. Although this is certainly a way to increase profits, it does not foster good relationships with artists/songwriters and should be avoided unless there is a good reason for taking this approach.

O. Reversion

Although the publisher takes the rights to all songs written by the composer, if the publisher cannot make use of any given song, it doesn't do either party much good for the publisher to keep it. Therefore, as long as the composer has repaid all advances, the composer can reclaim the rights to any composition for which the publisher has not secured a cover recording before the agreement expires.

> *If Publisher fails to secure a cover recording of the Compositions within the term of this Agreement, writer may, during the fifteen (15) days following the expiration of said term, demand the return of the Compositions in writing and if Publisher receives such notice within said fifteen (15) day time period, Publisher agrees to promptly reassign the compositions and all Publisher's rights therein to Writer and to execute any documents necessary to effect such reconveyance. Notwithstanding the foregoing, Publisher shall not be obliged to reassign the Compositions to Writer until such time as Writer shall repay to Publisher any advances or unrecouped demonstration recording costs chargeable to Writer.*

Conclusion

The examples presented in this book are the most common relationships between songwriter and publisher, although other, less formal arrangements certainly exist. Regardless of the arrangement, however, you should be aware that publishing income is one of the most significant sources of income available, so you should take care to understand it. To an independent record label, publishing is a significant source of income that should be considered when signing a new artist, whether the label asks for all or just a portion of the publishing.

Now that you understand how songwriters and publishers work together, we'll take a look at how publishers jointly own and promote compositions.

Form
Exclusive Songwriter Agreement

THIS AGREEMENT made and entered into this _____ day of _____, 20__ by and between Publishing Company (herein referred to as "Publisher") and John J. Songwriter (hereinafter referred to as "Writer".)

For and in consideration of the mutual convenants herein set forth, the parties hereby agree as follows:

1. EMPLOYMENT:

Publisher hereby employs Writer to render Writer's services as a songwriter and composer and otherwise as may hereinafter be set forth. Writer hereby accepts such employment and agrees to render such services exclusively for Publisher during the term hereof, upon the terms and conditions set forth herein.

2. TERM:

The initial term of this Agreement shall commence as of _____ and shall continue through _____. Writer hereby grants to Publisher _____ separate and irrevocable options, each to renew this Agreement for a one (1) year term, such renewal terms to run consecutively beginning at the expiration of the initial term hereof, all upon the same terms and conditions as are applicable to the initial term except as otherwise provided herein. Each option shall be exercised only by written notice to be sent by Publisher to Writer not less than ten (10) days prior to the commencement of the renewal term for which the option is exercised.

3. GRANT OF RIGHTS:

Writer hereby irrevocably and absolutely assigns, conveys and grants to Publisher, its successors and assigns (a) all rights and interests of every kind, nature and description in and to all original musical compositions and all original arrangements of musical compositions in the public domain which have heretofore been written, composed or created by Writer, in whole or in part, alone or in collaboration with others, including but not limited to the titles, lyrics and music thereof and all world-wide copyrights and renewals and extensions thereof under any present or future laws throughout the world, to the extent any of the foregoing shall not heretofore have been conveyed by Writer to an unrelated third party; and (b) all rights and interests of every kind, nature and description in and to the results and proceeds of Writer's services hereunder, including but not limited to the titles, lyrics and music of all original musical compositions and of all original arrangements of musical compositions in the public domain and all world-wide copyrights and renewals and extensions thereof under any present or future laws throughout the world, which shall be written, composed or created by Writer during the term hereof, in whole or in part, alone or in collaboration with others; and (c) all rights and interests of every kind, nature and description in and to all original musical compositions and all original arrangements of musical compositions in the public domain which are now directly or indirectly owned or controlled by Writer, in whole or in part, alone or with others, or the direct or indirect ownership or control of which shall be acquired by Writer during the term hereof, in whole or in part, alone or with others, as the employer or transferee of the writers or composers thereof or otherwise, including the titles, lyrics and music thereof and all world-wide copyrights and renewals and extensions thereof under any present or future laws throughout the world; all of which musical compositions, arrangements, rights and interests Writer hereby warrants and represents are and shall at all times be Publisher's exclusive property as the sole owner thereof, free from any adverse claims or rights therein by any other party (all such musical compositions and arrangements hereinafter being referred to as "Compositions.")

Without limiting the generality of the foregoing, Writer acknowledges that the rights and interests hereinabove set forth include Writer's irrevocable grant to Publisher, its successors and assigns, of the sole and exclusive right, license, privilege and authority throughout the entire world with respect to all Compositions, whether now in existence or whether created during the term hereof, as follows:

a.   To perform and license others to perform the Compositions publicly or privately, for profit or otherwise, by means of public or private performance, radio broadcast, television, or any and all other means of media, whether now known or hereafter conceived or developed.

b.   To substitute a new title or titles for the Compositions or any of them and to make any arrangement, adaptation, translation, dramatization or transposition of any or all of the Compositions or of the titles, lyrics or music thereof, in whole or in part, and in connection with any other musical, literary or dramatic material, and to add new lyrics to the music of any Compositions or new music to the lyrics of any Compositions, all as Publisher may deem necessary or desirable in its best business judgment.

c. To secure copyright registration and protection of the Compositions in Publisher's name or otherwise, as Publisher may desire, at Publisher's own cost and expense, and at Publisher's election, including any and all renewals and extensions of copyright under any present or future laws throughout the world, and to have and to hold said copyrights, renewals and extensions and all rights existing thereunder, for and during the full term of all said copyrights and all renewals and extensions and all rights existing thereunder, for and during the full term of all said copyrights and all renewals and extensions thereof.

d. To make or cause to be made, and to license others to make, master records, transcriptions, soundtracks, pressings and any other mechanical, electrical or other reproductions of the Compositions, in whole or in part, in such form or manner and as frequently as Publisher shall determine, including the right to synchronize the Compositions with sound motion pictures and to use, manufacture, advertise, license or sell such reproductions for any and all purposes, including, without limitation private and public performances, radio broadcast, television, sound motion pictures, wired radio, phonograph records and any and all other means or devices, whether now known or hereafter conceived or developed.

e. To print, publish and sell, and to license others to print, publish and sell, sheet music, orchestrations, arrangements and other editions of the Compositions in all forms, including, without limitation, the inclusion of any or all of the Compositions in song folios, compilations, song books, mixed folios, personality folios and lyric magazines with or without music.

f. Any and all other rights now or hereafter existing in all Compositions under and by virtue of any common law rights and all copyrights and renewals and extensions thereof including so-called small performance rights. Writer grants to Publisher, without any compensation other than as specified herein, the perpetual right to use and publish and to permit others to use and publish Writer's name (including any professional name heretofore or hereafter adopted by Writer), Writer's photograph or other likeness, or any reproduction or simulation thereof, and biographical material concerning Writer, and the titles of any and all of the Compositions, in connection with the printing, sale, advertising, performance, distribution and other exploitation of the Compositions, and for any other purpose related to the business of Publisher, its affiliated and related companies, or to refrain therefrom. This right shall be exclusive during the term hereof and nonexclusive thereafter. Writer shall not authorize or permit the use of Writer's name or likeness, or any reproduction or simulation thereof, or biographical material concerning Writer, for or in connection with any musical compositions, other than by or for Publisher. Writer grants Publisher the right to refer to Writer as Publisher's "Exclusive Songwriter and Composer" or to use any other similar and appropriate appellation, during the term hereof.

4.   EXCLUSIVITY:

During the term of this Agreement, Writer shall not write or compose, or furnish or convey, any musical compositions, titles, lyrics or music, or any rights or interests therein, nor participate in any manner with regard to same, for or to any party other than Publisher, nor permit the use of his name or likeness as the writer or co-writer of any musical composition by any party other than Publisher.

5.   WARRANTIES, REPRESENTATIONS, COVENANTS AND AGREEMENTS:

Writer hereby warrants, represents, covenants and agrees as follows: Writer has the full right, power and authority to enter into and perform this Agreement and to grant to and vest in Publisher all rights herein set forth, free and clear of any and all claims, rights and obligations whatsoever; all of the Compositions and all other results and proceeds of the services of Writer hereunder, including all of the titles, lyrics and music of the Compositions and each and every part thereof, delivered and to be delivered by Writer hereunder are and shall be new and original and capable of copyright protection throughout the entire world; no Composition shall, either in whole or in part, be an imitation or copy of, or infringe upon, any other material, or violate or infringe upon any common law or statutory rights of any party including, without limitation, contractual rights, copyrights and rights of privacy; and Writer has not sold, assigned, leased, licensed or in any other way disposed of or encumbered any Composition, in whole or in part, or any rights herein granted to Publisher, nor shall Writer sell, assign, lease, license or in any other way dispose of or encumber any of the Compositions, in whole or in part, or any of said rights, except under the terms and conditions hereof.

6.   POWER OF ATTORNEY:

Writer hereby irrevocably constitutes, authorizes, empowers and appoints Publisher or any of its officers Writer's true and lawful attorney (with full power of substitution and delegation), in Writer's name, and in Writer's place and stead, or in Publisher's name, to take and do such action, and to make, sign, execute, acknowledge and deliver any and all instruments or documents, which Publisher from time to time may deem desirable or necessary to vest in Publisher, its successors and assigns, all of the rights or interests granted by Writer hereunder, including, without limitation, such documents as Publisher shall deem desirable or necessary to secure to Publisher, its successors and assigns, the worldwide copyrights for all Compositions for the entire term of copyright and for any and all renewals and extensions under any present or future laws throughout the world. Notwithstanding the foregoing, Writer acknowledges that he (or she) is Publisher's employee for hire, that all Compositions are and shall be works made for hire and that Publisher is accordingly the author of all Compositions for all purposes of the 1909 or 1976 Copyright Law or any succeeding Copyright Law.

7.   COMPENSATION:

Provided that Writer shall duly perform the terms, covenants and conditions of this Agreement, Publisher shall pay Writer, for the services to be rendered by Writer hereunder and for the rights acquired and to be acquired by Publisher hereunder, the following compensation based on the Compositions

a.   Six cents ($.06) per copy for each copy of sheet music in standard piano/vocal notation and each dance orchestration printed, published and sold in the United States and Canada by Publisher or its licensees, for which payment shall have been received by Publisher, after deduction of returns.

b.   Ten percent (10%) of the wholesale selling price of each printed copy of each other arrangement and edition printed, published and sold in the United States and Canada by Publisher or its licensees, for which payment shall have been received by Publisher, after deduction of returns, except that in the event that any Compositions shall be used or caused to be used, in whole or in part, in conjunction with one or more other musical compositions in a folio, compilation, song book or other publication, Writer shall be entitled to receive that proportion of the foregoing royalty which the number of Compositions contained therein shall bear to the total number of musical compositions therein.

c. Fifty percent (50%) of any and all net sums actually received (less any costs for collection) by Publisher in the United States from the exploitation in the United States and Canada by licensees of mechanical rights, electrical transcription and reproduction rights, motion picture and television synchronization rights, dramatization rights and all other rights therein (except print rights, which are covered in (a) and (b) above, and public performance rights, which are covered in (d) below), whether or not such licensees are affiliated with, owned in whole or in part by, or controlled by Publisher.

d. Writer shall receive his public performance royalties throughout the world directly from the performing rights society with which he is affiliated, and shall have no claim whatsoever against Publisher for any royalties received by Publisher from any performing rights society which makes payment directly (or indirectly other than through Publisher) to writers, authors and composers. If, however, Publisher shall collect both the Writer's and Publisher's share of performance income directly and such income shall not be collected by Writer's public performance society, Publisher shall pay to Writer fifty percent (50%) of all such net sums which are received by Publisher in the United States from the exploitation of such rights in the Compositions, throughout the world.

e. Fifty percent (50%) of any and all net sums, after deduction of foreign taxes, actually received (less any costs for collection) by Publisher in the United States from the exploitation of the Compositions in countries outside of the United States and Canada (other than public performance royalties, which are covered in (d) above), whether from collection agents, licensees, subpublishers or others, and whether or not same are affiliated with, owned in whole or in part by, or controlled by Publisher.

f. Publisher shall not be required to pay any royalties on professional or complimentary printed copies or records or on printed copies or records which are distributed gratuitously to performing artists, orchestra leaders and disc jockeys or for advertising, promotional or exploitation purposes. Furthermore, no royalties shall be payable to Writer on consigned copies unless paid for, and not until such time as an accounting therefor can properly be made.

g. Royalties as hereinabove specified shall be payable solely to Writer in instances where Writer is the sole author of a Composition, including the lyrics and music thereof. However, in the event that one or more other songwriters are authors together with Writer of any Composition (including songwriters employed by Publisher to add, change or translate the lyrics or to revise or change the music), the foregoing royalties shall be divided equally among Writer and the other songwriters unless another division of royalties shall be agreed upon in writing between the parties concerned and timely written notice of such division is submitted to Publisher prior to payment.

h. Except as herein expressly provided, no other royalties or monies shall be paid to Writer.

i. Writer agrees and acknowledges that Publisher shall have the right to withhold from the royalties payable to Writer hereunder such amount, if any, as may be required under the provisions of all applicable Federal, State and other tax laws and regulations, and Writer agrees to execute such forms and other documents as may be required in connection therewith.

j. In no event shall Writer be entitled to share in any advance payments, guarantee payments or minimum royalty payments which Publisher shall receive in connection with any subpublishing agreement, collection agreement, licensing agreement or other agreement covering the Compositions or any of them.

8. ACCOUNTING:

Publisher shall compute the royalties earned by Writer pursuant to this Agreement and pursuant to any other agreement between Writer and Publisher or its affiliates, whether now in existence or entered into at any time subsequent hereto, on or before March 31st for the semiannual period ending the preceding December 31st and on or before September 30th for the semiannual period ending the preceding June 30th, and shall thereupon submit to Writer the royalty statement for each such period together with the net amount of royalties, if any, which shall be payable after deducting any and all unrecouped advances and chargeable costs under this Agreement or any such other agreement. Each statement submitted by Publisher to Writer shall be binding upon Writer and not subject to any objection by Writer for any reason unless specific written objection, stating the basis thereof, is sent by Writer to Publisher within one (1) year after the date said statement is submitted. Writer or a certified public accountant in Writer's behalf may, at Writer's expense, at reasonable intervals (but not more frequent than once each year), examine Publisher's books insofar as same concern Writer, during Publisher's usual business hours and upon reasonable notice, for the purpose of verifying the accuracy of any statement submitted to Writer hereunder. Publisher's books relating to activities during any accounting period may only be examined as aforesaid during the two (2) year period following service by Publisher of the statement for said accounting period.

9. COLLABORATION:

Whenever Writer shall collaborate with any other person in the creation of a Composition, the Composition shall be subject to the terms and conditions of this Agreement, and Writer warrants, represents and agrees that prior to such collaboration Writer shall advise such other person of this exclusive Agreement and shall further advise such other person that all Compositions so created must be published and owned by Publisher. In the event of any such collaboration, Writer shall notify Publisher of the nature and extent of such other person's contribution to the Composition, and Writer shall cause such other person to execute a separate songwriter's agreement with Publisher covering the Composition, which agreement shall set forth the division of the songwriter's royalties between Writer and such other person, and Publisher shall make payment accordingly.

10. SEPARATE AGREEMENTS:

If Publisher so desires, Publisher may request Writer to execute a separate agreement in Publisher's customary form with respect to each Composition hereunder. Upon such request, Writer shall promptly execute and deliver such separate agreement, and upon Writer's failure to do so, Publisher shall have the right, pursuant to the terms and conditions hereof, to execute such separate agreement in behalf of Writer. Such separate agreement shall supplement and not supersede this Agreement. In the event of any conflict between the provisions of such separate agreement and this Agreement, the provisions of this Agreement shall govern. The failure of either of the parties hereto to execute such separate agreement, whether such execution is requested by Publisher or not, shall not affect the rights of each of the parties hereunder, including but not limited to the rights of Publisher to all of the Compositions written, composed or acquired by Writer during the term hereof.

11. WRITER'S SERVICES:

a. Writer shall perform his required services hereunder conscientiously, and solely and exclusively for and as requested by Publisher. Writer is a writer for hire hereunder, and all Compositions are acknowledged by Writer to be works made for hire. Writer shall duly comply with all requirements and requests made by Publisher in connection with its business as set forth herein. Writer shall deliver a manuscript copy or tape copy of each Composition immediately upon the completion or acquisition of such Composition. Publisher shall use its reasonable efforts in its best business judgment to exploit all Compositions hereunder, but Publisher's failure to exploit any or all of said Compositions shall not be deemed a breach hereof. Publisher at its sole discretion shall reasonably make studio facilities available for Writer so that Writer, subject to the supervision and control of Publisher, may produce demonstration records of the Compositions, and Writer shall have the right to perform at such recording sessions. Publisher shall also have the right to produce demonstration records hereunder. Writer shall not incur any liability for which Publisher shall be responsible in connection with any demonstration record session without having obtained Publisher's prior written approval as to the nature, extent and limit of such liability. In no event shall Writer incur any expense whatsoever on behalf of Publisher without having obtained prior written authorization from Publisher. Writer shall not be entitled to any compensation (except for such compensation as is otherwise provided for herein) with respect to services rendered in connection with any such demonstration record sessions. Publisher shall advance the costs for the production of demonstration records, subject to the foregoing, and one-half (1/2) of such costs shall be deemed additional advances to Writer hereunder and shall be recouped by Publisher from royalties payable to Writer by Publisher under this Agreement or any other agreement between Writer and Publisher or its affiliates. All recordings and reproductions made at demonstration record sessions hereunder shall become the sole and exclusive property of Publisher, free of any claims whatsoever by Writer or any person deriving any rights from Writer.

b. Writer shall, from time to time, at Publisher's reasonable request, and whenever same will not unreasonably interfere with prior professional engagements of Writer, appear for photography, artwork and other similar purposes under the direction of Publisher or its duly authorized agent, appear for interviews and other promotional purposes, and confer and consult with Publisher or its duly authorized agent, appear for interviews and other promotional purposes, and confer and consult with Publisher regarding Writer's services hereunder. Writer shall also cooperate with Publisher in promoting, publicizing and exploiting the Compositions and for any other purpose related to the business of Publisher. Writer shall not be entitled to any compensation (other than applicable union scale if appropriate) for rendering such services, but shall be entitled to reasonable transportation and living expenses if such expenses must be incurred in order to render such services.

12. UNIQUE SERVICES:

Writer acknowledges that the services to be rendered by Writer hereunder are of a special, unique, unusual, extraordinary and intellectual character which gives them a peculiar value, the loss of which cannot be reasonably or adequately compensated in damages in an action at law, and that a breach by Writer of any of the provisions of this Agreement will cause Publisher great and irreparable injury and damage. Writer expressly agrees that Publisher shall be entitled to the remedies of injunction and other equitable relief to enforce this Agreement or to prevent a breach of this Agreement or any provision hereof, which relief shall be in addition to any other remedies, for damages or otherwise, which may be available to Publisher.

13. ACTIONS:

Publisher shall have the exclusive right to take such action as it deems necessary, either in Writer's name or in its own name or in both names, against any party to protect all rights and interests acquired by Publisher hereunder. Writer shall, cooperate fully with Publisher in any controversy which may arise or litigation which may be brought concerning Publisher's rights and interests acquired hereunder. Publisher shall have the right, in its discretion, to employ attorneys and to institute or defend against any claim, action or proceeding, whether for infringement of copyright or otherwise, and to take any other necessary steps to protect the right, title and interest of Publisher in and to each

Composition and, in connection therewith, to settle, compromise or in any other manner dispose of any such claim, action or proceeding and to satisfy or collect on any judgment which may be rendered. If Publisher shall recover on a judgment or as a result of a settlement with respect to any claim, action or proceeding for copyright infringement initiated by Publisher, all of Publisher's expenses in connection therewith, including, without limitation, attorney's fees and other costs, shall first be deducted, and fifty percent (50%) of the net proceeds shall be credited to Writer's account.

14. INDEMNITY:

Writer hereby indemnifies, saves and holds Publisher, its successors and assigns, harmless from any and all liability, claims, demands, loss and damage (including counsel fees and court costs) arising out of or connected with any claim or action by a third party which is inconsistent with any of the warranties, representations or agreements made by Writer in this Agreement, and Writer shall reimburse Publisher, on demand, for any loss, cost, expense or damage to which said indemnity applies. Publisher shall give Writer prompt written notice of any claim or action covered by said indemnity, and Writer shall have the right, at Writer's expense, to participate in the defense of any such claim or action with counsel of Writer's choice. Pending the disposition of any such claim or action, Publisher shall have the right to withhold payment of such portion of any monies which may be payable by Publisher to Writer under this Agreement or under any other agreement between Writer and Publisher or its affiliates as shall be reasonably related to the amount of the claim and estimated counsel fees and costs. If Publisher shall settle or compromise any such claim or action, the foregoing indemnity shall cover only that portion (if any) of the settlement or compromise which shall have been approved in writing by Writer, and Writer hereby agrees not unreasonably to withhold any such approval. Notwithstanding the foregoing, if Writer shall withhold approval of any settlement or compromise which Publisher is willing to make upon advice of counsel and in its best business judgment, Writer shall thereupon deliver to Publisher an indemnity or surety bond, in form satisfactory to Publisher, which shall cover the amount of the claim and estimated counsel fees and costs, and if Writer shall fail to deliver such bond within ten (10) business days, Writer shall be deemed to have approved of said settlement or compromise.

15. NOTICES:

Any written notices which Publisher shall desire to give to Writer hereunder, and all statements, royalties and other payments which shall be due to Writer hereunder, shall be addressed to Writer at the address set forth at the beginning of this agreement until Writer shall give Publisher written notice of a new address. All notices which Writer shall desire to give to Publisher hereunder shall be addressed to Publisher at the address set forth at the beginning of this agreement until Publisher shall give Writer written notice of a new address. All notices shall either be served by hand (to an officer of Publisher if Publisher shall be the addressee) or by registered or certified mail, postage prepaid, charges prepaid, addressed as aforesaid. The date of making personal service or of mailing, whichever shall be first, shall be deemed the date of service.

16. ENTIRE AGREEMENT:

This Agreement supersedes any and all prior negotiations, understandings and agreements between the parties hereto with respect to the subject matter hereof. Each of the parties acknowledges and agrees that neither party has made any representations or promises in connection with this Agreement or the subject matter hereof not contained herein.

17. MODIFICATION, WAIVER, INVALIDITY, AND CONTROLLING LAW:

This Agreement may not be cancelled, altered, modified, amended or waived, in whole or in part, in any way, except by an instrument in writing signed by the party sought to be bound. The waiver by either party of any breach of this Agreement in any one or more instances shall in no way be construed as a waiver of any subsequent breach of this Agreement (whether or not of a similar nature.) If any part of this Agreement shall be held to be void, invalid or unenforceable, it shall not affect the validity of the balance of this Agreement. This Agreement shall be deemed to have been made in the State of _____, and its validity, construction and effect shall be governed by the laws of the State of _____ applicable to agreements wholly performed therein. This Agreement shall not be binding upon Publisher until signed by Writer and countersigned by a duly authorized officer of Publisher.

18. ASSIGNMENT:

Publisher shall have the right to assign this Agreement or any of its rights hereunder to any party which is or shall be a subsidiary, affiliate or parent or to any party which shall acquire all or a substantial portion of Publisher's stock or assets.

19. DEFINITIONS:

For the purposes of this Agreement, "party" means and refers to any individual, corporation, partnership, association or any other organized group of persons or the legal successors or representatives of the foregoing. Whenever the expression "the term of this Agreement" or words of similar connotation are used herein, they shall be deemed to mean and refer to the initial term of this Agreement and any and all renewals, extensions, substitutions or replacements of this Agreement, whether expressly indicated or otherwise.

20. SUSPENSION AND TERMINATION:

If Writer shall fail, refuse or be unable to submit to Publisher new Compositions upon a reasonably regular schedule during each year of the Term hereof, or shall otherwise fail, refuse or be unable to perform his material obligations hereunder, Publisher shall have the right, in addition to all of its other rights and remedies at law or in equity, to suspend the term of this Agreement and its obligations hereunder by written notice to Writer, or, in the event such failure, refusal or inability shall continue for longer than six (6) months, to terminate this Agreement by written notice to Writer. Any such suspension shall continue for the duration of any such failure, refusal or inability, and, unless Publisher notifies Writer to the contrary in writing, the then current term hereof shall be automatically extended by the number of days which shall equal the total number of days of suspension. During any such suspension Writer shall not render services as a songwriter and/or composer to any other party or assign, license or convey any musical composition to any other party.

21. HEADING:

The heading of clauses or other divisions hereof are inserted only for the purpose of convenient reference. Such headings shall not be deemed to govern, limit, modify or in any other manner affect the scope, meaning or intent of the provisions of this Agreement or any part thereof, nor shall they otherwise be given any legal effect.

[[22. ANNUAL PAYMENTS:

Conditioned upon, and in consideration of, the full and faithful performance by Writer of all of the terms and provisions hereof, Publisher shall pay to Writer the following amounts, in equal monthly installments, all of which shall be recoupable by Publisher from any and all royalties payable to Writer under this or any other agreement between Writer and Publisher and from any and all monies payable to Writer's designee under the Participation Agreement described in clause 23 below:

a.   during the initial term hereof.

b.   during the first renewal term (if any).

c.   during the second renewal term (if any)

d.   during the third renewal term (if any)

e.   during the fourth renewal term (if any)]]

23. RECOUPMENT:

It is understood and acknowledged that any and all charges or advances against royalties under this agreement which are not recouped by Publisher may be recouped by Publisher's record company affiliate or its assignee from any and all royalties earned by Writer under the aforementioned recording contract or its successor or replacement agreement, and that any and all charges or advances against royalties under said recording contract or its successor or replacement agreement which are not recouped by said record company or its assignee may be recouped by Publisher from any and all royalties earned by Writer hereunder.

24. REVERSION:

If Publisher fails to secure a cover recording of the Compositions within the term of this Agreement, writer may, during the fifteen (15) days following the expiration of said term, demand the return of the Compositions in writing and if Publisher receives such notice within said fifteen (15) day time period, Publisher agrees to promptly reassign the compositions and all Publisher's rights therein to Writer and to execute any documents necessary to effect such reconveyance. Notwithstanding the foregoing, Publisher shall not be obliged to reassign the Compositions to Writer until such time as Writer shall repay to Publisher any advances or unrecouped demonstration recording costs chargeable to Writer.

Chapter 4

Two (or More) Publishers
Are Better Than One:
Co-Publishing Arrangements

Many times two or more publishers will jointly publish a composition. The resulting agreement between the parties differ, depending on how much responsibility each publisher takes on. In this chapter, we'll review co-publishing agreements. In a co-publishing agreement, each publisher will own a percentage of the copyright and each will promote the song. However, one company will assume the responsibility for administering the song (that is, collecting and distributing the royalties, filing the copyrights and work registrations, etc.).

This arrangement is very common when an artist signs with a record label that wishes to assume a portion of the artist's publishing. If the artist negotiates well with the record company, the artist retains his or her publishing, then later (and for an additional advance) transfers a portion of the publishing to the record company's publishing affiliate. If the artist negotiates fairly well with the record company, the artist and the record company will divide the publishing as part of the record deal. (An artist that negotiates poorly will turn over all publishing as part of the record deal). For independent labels, especially, retaining a portion of the publishing and co-publishing with the artist is very common. Small independent labels generally have a shortage of cash flow that requires them to seek additional income streams in order to make a deal profitable.

To illustrate, let's return to our example. Suppose that, Fred, Joe and Bob, as the rock band Groove Therapy, sign a deal with Livin' Large Records. As before, assume Livin' Large is a small label that needs additional income streams to assist it in properly promoting the album. However, assume now that Fred, Joe and Bob are a little more careful in their negotiations and, instead of turning all publishing over to the label's affiliate, Uptown, they decide to retain half of their publishing. They wish to equally share their portion of the publishing, so Fred, Joe and Bob form a single publisher that they each own equally, Sky's the Limit Publishing. Through a non-exclusive songwriting agreement, Fred, Joe and Bob each assign all of their publishing (and copyrights) to Sky's the Limit, meaning that Fred, Joe and Bob, own all songwriting and through their publisher, the copyright and publishing. Sky's the Limit then enters into a co-publishing arrangement with Uptown. Through the co-publishing agreement, Sky's the Limit and Uptown will share in the publishing income and ownership, but all songwriting income will still go to Fred, Joe and Bob as individuals.

A co-publishing arrangement is also common, although sometimes less formal, when two or more songwriters collaborate and each retains his or her publishing. If Fred, Joe and Bob had each formed their own publishing company, rather than owning Sky's the Limit together, their publishing companies could co-publish.

Biz Note: Some independent labels insist upon taking 100% of the publishing for any song that their artist songwriters compose. This is not as common as a 50/50 split, but it does happen. As you will see, the record label's publisher is generally responsible for all of the administrative tasks (copyrights, registrations, licensing, accounting). Record label publishers frequently cite this as justification for demanding all publishing rights. Although it appears that the work load is unfairly divided if the record company's publisher takes all of the work and only half of the income, the artist/songwriter is, in fact, performing a publishing function. Since the songwriter is a recording artist, the songwriter is actually promoting the songs in the publishing catalog by placing them on an album that is being distributed to the public (which frequently results in other artists requesting permission to do "covers"). This is justification for a split, rather than full conveyance to the record company's publisher, although it largely turns on the record company's wishes and the artist's bargaining power.

A. Ownership

This example provides that two publishers will own the copyright equally. However, the publishers can split the percentages any way they choose.

> *Company and Participant shall jointly own the Composition, in equal shares, including all of the worldwide right, title and interest,*

including the copyrights, the right to copyright and the renewal rights, therein and thereto.

Biz note: Although a 50/50 split is probably the most common arrangement, it is also common for the record company to split 75/25 (songwriter/record label publisher) for an artist that has some serious selling power. It is equally as common for the record company to split 25/75 (songwriter/record label publisher) for an artist that has less of a track record.

B. Registration

Although both own the composition, the copyright is held in the name of the publisher designated as the "Company," who is to be the administrator.

> *The Composition shall be registered for copyright by Company in the name of Company in the office of the Register of Copyrights of the United States of America and Company shall take all reasonable measures to protect the copyright in the Composition in those territories which are signatories to the Universal Copyright Convention. If the Composition has heretofore been registered for copyright in the name of Participants, Participants shall simultaneously herewith deliver to Company an assignment of a one-half interest therein, in form acceptable to Company.*

C. Administration

Because the Company is the administrator, it is the publisher responsible for all of the paperwork. That includes granting licenses for others to use the work. Under this type of arrangement, the "Participant" publisher cannot issue licenses because the "Company" publisher is managing, and collecting royalties for, the composition. Such management frequently means that the Company publisher must be aware of (and therefore in control of) all licensing.

> *Company shall have the sole and exclusive right to administer and exploit the Composition, to print, publish, sell, use and license the use of the Composition throughout the world, and to execute in its own name any and all licenses and agreements affecting or respecting the Composition, including without limitation licenses for mechanical reproduction, public performance, synchronization uses, subpublication, merchandising, and advertising and to assign or license such rights*

to others. This statement of exclusive rights is only in clarification and amplification of the rights of Company hereunder and not in limitation thereof.

D. Royalties

As noted above, the Company publisher collects all monies from licensing fees and other sources, and pays all costs associated with administering the song.

> *Company shall be entitled to receive and collect and shall receive and collect all gross receipts derived from the Composition. "Gross Receipts," as used herein, shall mean any and all revenue, income and sums derived from the Composition from any and all sources whatsoever.*

After costs, the Company publisher pays the Participant publisher its share of the proceeds, here half. The costs include overhead:

> *A sum equal to ten percent (10%) of the Gross Receipts as an administration charge for overhead.*

writers royalties:

> *Royalties and other sums which are paid by Company to the composers and writers of the Composition pursuant to the provisions of the songwriter's agreements between either publisher hereunder and such composers and writers, or which, at Company's election, are paid by Company to Participant, in trust, for payment over by Participant to such composers and writers pursuant to the provisions of said songwriter's agreements.*

collection costs:

> *Collection or other fees customarily and actually charged by any collection agent which may be used by Company.*

out of pocket costs:

> *Actual, out of pocket administrative and exploitation expenses of Company with respect to the Composition for registration fees,*

advertising and promotion expenses directly related to the Composition, the costs of transcribing for lead sheets, and the costs of producing demonstration recordings.

attorneys' fees:

Attorneys' fees directly related to the defense of claims respecting the Composition, if any, actually paid by Company.

and print costs:

The costs of printing, engraving, arranging and editing printed editions of the Composition incurred by Company.

E. Performance rights

The agreement will set forth which performance society is to be used, here BMI, although this will depend upon the society that the particular publisher is a member of. Unlike songwriter agreements, the Company Publisher will collect all performance royalties and remit Participant's share to the participant. This is because the performance rights societies have rules concerning the collection of songwriter royalties that do not permit a company to collection on a songwriter's behalf. Those rules do not apply to publishing companies.

The performing rights in the Composition, to the extent permitted by law, shall be assigned to and licensed by Broadcast Music, Inc. (BMI). BMI shall be and hereby is authorized to collect and receive all moneys earned from the public performance of the Composition and to pay directly to Company one hundred percent (100%) of the amount allocated by BMI as the publisher's share of the public performance fees.

F. Mechanical Royalties

The Company publisher collects all mechanical royalties. Mechanical royalties are the royalties that a songwriter and publisher receive from a record company for permission to mechanically reproduce and distribute copies of the composition. Where the publisher is affiliated with the record company that will be recording and releasing the song, the Company publisher will frequently charge the highest rate for the composition (unless there is a recording artist agreement that provides otherwise) and waive the overhead.

> *Mechanical royalties for the Composition for the Untied States and Canada shall be collectible by Company or by any other collection agent which may be designated by Company, provided however, that Company shall, in the case of any record company affiliated with Company, issue the mechanical licenses directly to said record company at the then current statutory rate and collect mechanical royalties directly therefrom in which case there shall be no administration charge as referred to above.*

To illustrate, the author represents a number of independent record labels of various sizes. All of these labels, with no exception, have affiliated publishing companies. Furthermore, all of them, with no exception, take a portion of the publishing for each composition written by a label artist, as a condition to signing the artist. Therefore, unless the label takes all of the publishing, the label's publishing company and the songwriter's publishing company co-publish.

If the record company's publisher, Uptown (returning to our earlier example) discounted the rate by charging the record company only 75% of the going rate, this discount would, of course, increase the record company's profit. It would also reduce the publishing *and* songwriting income by 25%. Since the label and Uptown are both owned by the same people, what Uptown loses on the publishing end, it picks up through the record company. The songwriter and his publisher, though, just lost 25%. How fair is that, especially if Uptown charges a 10% overhead fee for providing this service? Therefore, where the Company publisher is "self-dealing," no discounts or administration fee are allowed, except for what has already been provided for under the recording agreement. Where the recording agreement provides that controlled compositions are to be licensed at a discount (for instance, 75% of the statutory rate), this rule would not apply.

G. Accounting

The Company publisher, as the party that collects all of the money, must issue statements to the Participant publisher, along with the participant's share of the income, similar to the songwriting agreements. The participant has a set amount of time to contest a statement, and a set amount of time to audit before it is foreclosed from doing so.

> *Statements as to monies payable hereunder shall be sent by Company to Participants seminannually within ninety (90) days after*

the end of each semiannual calendar period. Statements shall be accompanied by appropriate payments. Participants shall be deemed to have consented to all royalty statements and other accounts rendered by Company to Participants, and said statements and other accounts shall be binding upon Participant and not subject to any objection for any reason, unless specific objection in writing, setting forth the basis thereof, is given by Participant's to Company with two (2) years from the date rendered. Participants or a certified public accountant in its behalf may, at reasonable intervals, examine the books of Company pertaining to the Composition during Company's usual business hours and upon reasonable notice. Said books relating to activities and receipts during any accounting period may only be examined as aforesaid during the two (2) year period following service by Company of the statement for said accounting period only during Company's normal business hours and upon ten days written notice.

H. Indemnity

If each publisher has a songwriting agreement with a different songwriter, then the publishers will "share" indemnities.

> *Each party hereto shall give the other the equal benefits of any warranties or representations which it obtained or shall obtain under any agreements affecting the Composition.*

For instance, suppose Fred wrote some lyrics and Ethel later added music to complete the composition. Fred signed a songwriter agreement with Uptown and Ethel assigned her rights to Sideswipe Music. Sideswipe and Uptown then enter into a co-publishing agreement. After the song is recorded and released, someone accuses Fred of copying her lyrics, then sues Fred and both publishers. Since Sideswipe has no contract with Fred, it cannot force Fred to cover its losses because Fred made Sideswipe no guarantees. However, this provision gives Sideswipe the benefit of Fred's guarantees and indemnity to Uptown.

I. Defense of copyright

Because the company publisher is the administrator, it will want the right to defend any suit that is brought regarding the composition. This is especially true if the company publisher is the larger, more affluent publisher (that is, the one better capable of footing the bill to mount a thorough defense).

The participant publisher can, of course, participate in the defense, but must pay its own costs. If there is any recovery from any lawsuit, the publishers will split the proceeds, after deduction of costs.

> *Company shall have the sole right to prosecute, defend, settle and compromise all suits, claims, and actions respecting the composition, and generally to do and perform all things necessary concerning the same and the copyrights therein, to prevent and restrain the infringement of copyrights or other rights with respect to the Composition. In the event of the recovery by Company of any moneys as a result of a judgment or settlement, such moneys, less an amount equal to the expense of obtaining said moneys, including counsel fees, shall be deemed additional gross receipts hereunder. Participant shall have the right to provide counsel for itself, but at its own expense, to assist in any such manner. Company will not settle any claim respecting the Composition without Participants' consent, which consent shall not be unreasonably withheld.*

J. Term

The publishing agreement is intended to last for the life of the copyrights:

> *The rights of the parties hereto in and to the Composition shall extend for the term of the copyright of the Composition and of any derivative copyrights therein in the United States of America and throughout the rest of the world and for the terms of any renewals or extensions thereof in the United States of America and throughout the rest of the world.*

K. Warranties

The Participant publisher will generally have to make some promises to the Company publisher. Similar to other recording industry agreements, the company is "buying into" a certain package. If the facts are other than as represented to the company, then the package may not be worth as much (and the company may not have done the deal). Therefore, the participant must promise that it is not under any restriction that would prevent it from making this agreement. An example of this would be if the participant had already assigned the rights to another publisher. The participant must back this promise with an indemnity. The indemnity is yet another promise to cover any losses that the company might suffer if someone comes along and makes a claim to the composition. To illustrate, let's return to our example. Fred and Bob write a song, then assign the publishing to their own publishing company, FredBob Publishing. FredBob Publishing, as a small publisher, assigns half of the publishing to Uptown Music, a large publisher with an established promotions department. If Steve later accuses Fred and Bob of infringing his copyright, then sues Fred, Bob, FredBob Publishing and Uptown, Uptown will look to FredBob to repay any costs that Uptown pays, regardless of whether the case is won or lost.

> *Participants hereby warrants and represents that it has the right to enter into this agreement and to grant to Company all of the rights granted herein, and that the exercise by Company of any and all of the rights granted to Company in this agreement will not violate or infringe upon any common law or statutory rights of any person, firm or corporation, including, without limitation, contractual rights, copyrights and rights of privacy. The rights granted herein are free and clear of any claims, demands, liens or encumbrances. Participant agrees to and does hereby indemnity, save and hold Company, its assigns, licensees, and its and their directors, officers, shareholders, agents and employees harmless from any and all liabilities, claims, demands, loss and damage (including attorneys fees and court costs) arising out of or connected with any claim by a third party which is inconsistent with any of the warranties, representations, covenants, or agreements made by Participant herein and Participant agrees to reimburse Company, on demand, for any payment made by Company at any time after the date hereof with respect to any liability or claim to which the foregoing indemnity applies. Pending the determination of any such claim, Company may withhold payment of royalties or other moneys hereunder, provided that all amounts so withheld are reasonably related to the amount of said claim and the estimated attorneys' fees in connection therewith, and provided further that Participants shall have the right to post a bond in an amount reasonably satisfactory to Company by a bonding company reasonably satisfactory to company, in which events Company shall not withhold payments as aforesaid.*

The company can withhold royalties due the participant to pay company's costs *and* to build a reserve fund from which to pay any future costs. If the participant wants that money released, it can post a bond. However, you should note that a bond requires a premium of 10% of the face value, and requires collateral commensurate with the coverage. Notice, as well, that the amount of the bond is at the company's discretion.

L. Other paperwork

More often than not, the contract will not be the only document that the participant will ever have to sign. As we discussed in the previous chapter, the compositions are frequently licensed to numerous entities, and bought and traded with other publishers. Therefore, the company will want to make sure that the participant will sign whatever other documents are necessary to accomplish these tasks.

> *The parties hereto shall execute any further documents including, without limitation, assignments of copyrights, and do all acts necessary to fully effectuate the terms and provisions of this agreement.*

M. Subpublishing

Subpublishing refers to collecting publishing monies from foreign countries. The company publisher will want the right to enter into agreements with other publishers in order to collect foreign royalties.

> *Company may enter into subpublishing agreements with, or assign, or license any of its rights hereunder to, one or more other person, firms, or corporations for any one or more countries of the world. In the event Company enters into a subpublishing or administration agreement for any country of the world with a company affiliated with or otherwise related to Company, such agreement shall be deemed to have been made with an independent third party provided, that no foreign subpublishing agreement respecting the Composition shall be on terms less favorable to Company than what is commonly referred to in the music publishing industry and a 75/25/10 division of royalties and a 50/50/10 division with respect to so-called foreign cover records. Participant acknowledges that Company has the right to administer and publish compositions other than the Composition.*

Conclusion

Co-publishing arrangements can be very beneficial for both parties. The publisher with the experience and resources manages the catalog and realizes a substantial portion of the publishing income for its troubles. The publisher with less experience has the benefit of handing the minutia to another publisher, while avoiding handing over all of the income.

However, there are instances when a songwriter simply cannot bring himself to share publishing. Similarly, there are instances, especially in the world of independent labels, where the record label publisher will want to hand the bulk of the responsibilities to another company that has the time and manpower to devote to it. In the next chapter, we'll look at another alternative, the Administration Agreement.

Forms
Co-Publishing Agreement

THIS AGREEMENT made this _____ day of _____, 200__, by and between _____ (hereinafter referred to as "Company") and _____ (hereinafter referred to as "Participant")

WHEREAS, it is the intention of Company and Participant that they shall jointly own, in equal shares, the musical composition entitled _____ (hereinafter referred to as the "Composition") listed or described below, so that 50% of the entire worldwide right, title and interest, including the copyright, the right to copyright and the renewal right, in and to the Composition shall be owned by Company and 50% thereof shall be owned by Participant;

WHEREAS, the Composition has been or shall be registered for copyright in the name of Company in the Copyright Office of the United States of America;

NOW, THEREFORE, for good and valuable consideration the receipt of which is hereby acknowledged by each party hereto, it is agreed as follows:

1. Company and Participant shall jointly own the Composition, in equal shares, including all of the worldwide right, title and interest, including the copyrights, the right to copyright and the renewal rights, therein and thereto.

2. The Composition shall be registered for copyright by Company in the name of Company in the office of the Register of Copyrights of the United States of America and Company shall take all reasonable measures to protect the copyright in the Composition in those territories which are signatories to the Universal Copyright Convention. If the Composition has heretofore been registered for copyright in the name of Participants, Participants shall simultaneously herewith deliver to Company an assignment of a one-half interest therein, in form acceptable to Company.

3. Company shall have the sole and exclusive right to administer and exploit the Composition, to print, publish, sell, use and license the use of the Composition throughout the world, and to execute in its own name any

and all licenses and agreements affecting or respecting the Composition, including but not limited to licenses for mechanical reproduction, public performance, synchronization uses, subpublication, merchandising, and advertising and to assign or license such rights to others. This statement of exclusive rights is only in clarification and amplification of the rights of Company hereunder and not in limitation thereof

4. Company shall be entitled to receive and collect and shall receive and collect all gross receipts derived from the Composition. "Gross receipts," as used herein, shall mean any and all revenue, income and sums derived from the Composition from any and all sources whatsoever.

5. Company shall pay to Participant 50% of the net income actually received and derived by Company from the Composition. "Net income," as used herein, shall mean the gross receipts derived by Company from the Composition, less the following;

    a. A sum equal to ten percent (10%) of the Gross Receipts as an administration charge for overhead.

    b. Royalties and other sums which are paid by Company to the composers and writers of the Composition pursuant to the provisions of the songwriter's agreements between Participants and such composers and writers (a copy of which is attached hereto as Exhibit "A") or which, at Company's election, are paid by Company to Participant, in trust, for payment over by Participant to such composers and writers pursuant to the provisions of said songwriter's agreements;

    c. Collection or other fees customarily and actually charged by or any other collection agent which may be used by Company;

    d. Actual, out-of-pocket administrative and exploitation expenses of company with respect to the Composition for registration fees, advertising and promotion expenses directly related to the Composition, the costs of transcribing for lead sheets, and the costs of producing demonstration records;

    e. Attorneys' fees directly related to the defense of claims respecting the Composition, if any, actually paid by Company;

    f. The costs of printing, engraving, arranging and editing printed editions of the Composition incurred by Company.

6. The performing rights in the Composition, to the extent permitted by law, shall be assigned to and licensed by Broadcast Music, Inc. (BMI). BMI shall be and hereby is authorized to collect and receive all moneys earned from the public performance of the Composition and to pay directly to Company one hundred percent (100%) of the amount allocated by BMI as the publisher's share of public performance fees.

7. Mechanical royalties for the Composition for the United States and Canada shall be collectible by or any other collection agent which may be designated by Company, provided however, that Company shall, in the case of any record company affiliated with Company, issue the mechanical licenses directly to said record company at the then current statutory rate and collect mechanical royalties directly therefrom in which case there shall be no collection fee as referred to in paragraph 5(c).

8. Statements as to moneys payable hereunder shall be sent by Company to Participants semiannually within ninety (90) days after the end of each semiannual calendar period. Statements shall be accompanied by appropriate payments. Participants shall be deemed to have consented to all royalty statements and other accounts rendered by Company to Participants, and said statements and other accounts shall be binding upon Participant and not subject to any objection for any reason, unless specific objection in writing, setting forth the basis thereof, is given by Participants to Company within two (2) years from the date rendered. Participants or a certified public accountant in its behalf may, at reasonable intervals, examine the books of Company pertaining to the Composition during Company's usual business hours and upon reasonable notice. Said books relating to activities and receipts during any accounting period may only be examined as aforesaid during the two (2) year period following service by Company of the statement for said accounting period only during Company's normal business hours and upon ten days written notice.

9. Each party hereto shall give the other the equal benefits of any warranties or representations which it obtained or shall obtain under any agreements affecting the Composition.

10. Company shall have the sole right to prosecute, defend, settle and compromise all suits, claims, and actions respecting the composition, and generally to do and perform all things necessary concerning the same and the copyrights therein, to prevent and restrain the infringement of copyrights

or other rights with respect to the Composition. In the event of the recovery by Company of any moneys as a result of a judgment or settlement, such moneys, less an amount equal to the expense of obtaining said moneys, including counsel fees, shall be deemed additional gross receipts hereunder. Participant shall have the right to provide counsel for itself, but at its own expense, to assist in any such manner. Company will not settle any claim respecting the Composition without Participants' consent, which consent shall not be unreasonably withheld.

11. The rights of the parties hereto in and to the Composition shall extend for the term of the copyright of the Composition and of any derivative copyrights therein in the United States of America and throughout the rest of the world and for the terms of any renewals or extensions thereof in the United States of America and throughout the rest of the world.

12. This agreement sets forth the entire understanding between the parties, and cannot be changed, modified or canceled except by an instrument signed by the party sought to be bound. This agreement shall be governed by and construed under the laws of the State of _____ applicable to agreements wholly performed therein.

13. Participants hereby warrants and represents that it has the right to enter into this agreement and to grant to Company all of the rights granted herein, and that the exercise by Company of any and all of the rights granted to Company in this agreement will not violate or infringe upon any common law or statutory rights of any person, firm or corporation, including, without limitation, contractual rights, copyrights and rights of privacy. The rights granted herein are free and clear of any claims, demands, liens or encumbrances. Participants agrees to and does hereby indemnity, save and hold Company, its assigns, licensees, and its and their directors, officers, shareholders, agents and employees harmless from any and all liabilities, claims, demands, loss and damage (including attorneys fees and court costs) arising out of or connected with any claim by a third party which is inconsistent with any of the warranties, representations, covenants, or agreements made by Participant herein and Participant agrees to reimburse Company, on demand, for any payment made by Company at any time after the date hereof with respect to any liability or claim to which the foregoing indemnity applies. Pending the determination of any such claim, Company may withhold payment of royalties or other moneys hereunder, provided that all amounts so withheld are reasonably related to the amount

of said claim and the estimated attorneys' fees in connection therewith, and provided further that Participants shall have the right to post a bond in an amount reasonably satisfactory to Company by a bonding company reasonably satisfactory to company, in which events Company shall not withhold payments as aforesaid.

14. All notices, statements or other documents which either party shall be required or shall desire to give to the other hereunder must be in writing and shall be given by the parties hereto only in one of the following ways: (1) by personal delivery; or (2) by addressing them as indicated below, and by depositing them postage prepaid, in the United States mail, airmail if the address is outside of the state in which such notice is deposited; or (3) by delivering them toll prepaid to a telegraph or cable company. If so delivered, mailed, telegraphed or cabled, each such notice, statement or other document shall, except as herein expressly provided, be conclusively deemed to have been given when personally delivered or on the date of delivery to the telegraph or cable company or 24 hours after the date of mailing, as the case may be. The addresses of the parties shall be those of which the other party actually receives written notice and until further notice are:

"Company"

_____   _____%
_____
_____

"Participant"

_____   _____%
_____
_____

This agreement shall not be deemed to give any right or remedy to any third party whatsoever unless said right or remedy is specifically granted to such third party by the terms hereof

16. The parties hereto shall execute any further documents including, without limitation, assignments of copyrights, and do all acts necessary to fully effectuate the terms and provisions of this agreement.

17. Company may enter into subpublishing agreements with, or assign, or license any of its rights hereunder to, one or more other person, firms, or corporations for any one or more countries of the world. In the event Company enters into a subpublishing or administration agreement for any country of the world with a company affiliated with or otherwise related to Company, such agreement shall be deemed to have been made with an independent third party provided, that no foreign subpublishing agreement respecting the Composition shall be on terms less favorable to Company than what is commonly referred to in the music publishing industry and a 75/25/10 division of royalties and a 50/50/10 division with respect to so-called foreign cover records. Participant acknowledges that Company has the right to administer and publish compositions other than the Composition.

IN WITNESS WHEREOF, the parties have executed this agreement the day and year above set forth.

Chapter 5

Downloading the Details: Administration Agreements

There are other types of agreements between publishers, as well. Where the publishers enter into an administration agreement, the originating publisher will retain all rights in the composition, but the other publisher will promote and administer the composition. A songwriter who truly understands the income potential of publishing royalties will not want to give up any publishing if he or she does not absolutely have to. Although the bargaining power frequently favors the record company and its publisher, there are times when the songwriter brings enough to the table that the record company and its publisher may be willing to forgo publishing rights. However, the fact remains that many, many songwriters are not equipped to handle the administrative details that come with an income producing composition. Therefore, the songwriter and the record company's publisher may enter into an agreement whereby the record company's publisher agrees to administer the song for a fee, but takes no interest in the copyrights covered by the agreement. This also works well for record companies will large catalogs, but little manpower to manage them.

A. Duties

The publisher's role as administrator is similar to its publishing duties. It will register copyrights and registrations with the performance rights societies, promote the compositions, and issue licenses on behalf of the songwriter's publisher:

> *This agreement is made with respect to all musical compositions, heretofore or during the term hereof, written or composed, in whole or in part, or owned or controlled, directly or indirectly, by Publisher or*

any firm or corporation affiliated with or related to it or which it shall form, a complete schedule of which, as of the date hereof, is set forth on Schedule "A" attached hereto (such musical compositions being here-inafter referred to as the "Compositions"). During the term hereof, Administrator shall have the exclusive right to administer and exploit the Compositions throughout the world; to print, publish, sell, use and license the performance and use of the Compositions throughout the world; and to execute in Publisher's name any licenses and agreements affecting the Compositions, including, but not limited to, licenses for mechanical reproduction, public performance and synchronization uses, and to assign in the normal course of business or license all such rights to third parties. Administrator in its discretion or at the request of Publisher, and on receipt of all necessary information, shall register in the name of Publisher claims to copyright in the Compositions together with any other documents which Administrator deems necessary to register in the United States Copyright Office.

This clause illustrates one of the main differences between assigning publishing and merely allowing another company to administer. The copyright is retained in full by the songwriter's publisher, rather than being shared with the administrator.

The administrator's rights are exclusive. The songwriter's publisher may not issue licenses to other users for a number of reasons. An administrator must be able to track what rights are granted. For instance, assume Uptown Music is the administrator of Sky's the Limit's catalog of musical compositions. If Uptown grants a corporation the exclusive right to use a certain song for ads featuring software packages, then Sky's the Limit issues a license to another software company for that same song, then Sky's the Limit has just unknowingly stumbled into a breach of contract. Therefore, the administrator will reserve all rights to exploit the composition and collect the income, and all licenses must be issued by the administrator.

The administrator should also reserve the right to collect all money that is derived from the use of the compositions, with the exception of the writer's share of money paid by ASCAP, BMI or SESAC:

Administrator shall collect all gross receipts earned by and derived from the Compositions during the term hereof, regardless of when paid. "Gross receipts" is defined as any revenue derived from the Compositions less amounts paid to or deducted by foreign subpublishers, sublicensees, collection agencies and local performing and mechanical

rights societies. Gross receipts shall include, without limitation, mechan-
ical royalties, synchronization fees, print income and the "writer's" and
"publisher's share" of public performance income, provided, however,
that the composers of any Compositions hereunder shall have the right
to collect the "writer's share" of any such income directly from the appli-
cable performing rights society.

From the administrator's perspective, this point should be non-negotiable. The most practical reason is that if the administrator is tracking all of the licenses issued, the administrator is in a much better position to track whether all resulting money has been paid. Secondly, the administrator will have the systems in place to render proper accountings and pay out royalties, whereas the songwriter generally will not.

B. Compensation

For administering the compositions, the administering publisher will generally charge a percentage of revenues plus expenses as the fee for services.

For its services hereunder, Administrator shall be paid its reasonable
expenses, plus ten percent (10%) of the gross receipts derived from the
Compositions; provided, however, that Administrator shall be entitled
to twenty-five percent (25%) of the gross receipts derived from cover
recordings of the Compositions secured by Administrator. The term
"cover recording" shall mean any recording of a Composition by any
person other than the composer or composers of such Composition, or
placement of a Composition in a motion picture, television program or
commercial. In the event there shall be both cover records and other
records released of any Composition hereunder, then, for the purposes of
the computation of Administrator's fees, performance income with
respect to any such Composition shall be divided into two (2) categories
in the same proportion that mechanical income is earned during the
period that any such performance income is earned, and the applicable
percentages hereunder paid with respect to any such mechanical income
shall be paid with respect to each such category of performance income.

The fee schedule may differ depending on who records the composition. Here, if the composer releases the recording, the administrator receives 10% of the gross receipts. If, however, the administrator is able to secure a "cover" by another artist, the administrator will receive 25% of gross. There is also a formula for allocating performance income (that is, royalties paid by ASCAP, BMI and SESAC) if there are both a cover and a songwriter recorded version of the song.

In addition to the percentage fee, the administrator should recover all reasonable non-overhead expenses incurred in administrating the compositions:

> *"Reasonable expenses" are defined as the following: (i) actual out-of-pocket non-overhead administrative and exploitation expenses of Administrator with respect to the Compositions including, without limitation, registration fees, the costs of transcribing for lead sheets, and the costs of producing demonstration records to the extent such expenses are not recouped from the composer's royalties; provided, however Administrator shall incur no single expense in excess of Fifty Dollars ($50) without the consent of Publisher; and (ii) attorneys' fees, if any, actually paid by Administrator for any agreements (other than the present agreement) affecting the Compositions.*

C. Songwriter royalties

The administrator may also take over the responsibility of paying songwriter royalties to the composers, or it may elect to leave that responsibility to the publisher:

> *Songwriter royalties shall be paid to any composer (including Publisher, if applicable) of any Composition hereunder. Said royalties shall be paid pursuant to any songwriter agreement between any such composer and Publisher or Publisher's predecessor in interest, if any, and such accounting to any such composer (other than Publisher, if applicable) shall be on a semi-annual basis unless required otherwise by such agreement. True copies of any such agreement shall be promptly submitted by Publisher to Administrator. Administrator shall have the election of paying on Publisher's behalf any such composer such royalties or paying such royalties to Publisher, in trust, for payment over by Publisher to any such composer.*

Some administrators prefer to pay the songwriters directly to ensure that the songwriters are paid in a timely manner and don't look to the administrator for royalties already paid to the publisher. However, the record company's publisher should use caution in taking over the responsibility for paying songwriter royalties. If the terms of the agreement between the songwriter and the publisher differ from the administrator's standard procedure, there could be problems. For example, say Uptown pays royalties on a semi-annual basis. However, Sky's the Limit has agreed with its songwriter to issue statements on a quarterly basis. If Uptown takes over Sky's the Limit's duties to pay the songwriters, it must do so on Sky's the Limit's quarterly schedule, rather than its own semi-annual schedule. For some publishers, adjusting the schedule would not be a problem. For others, however, changes in routine procedures can be problematic, and this should be considered when deciding to whether to take over the responsibility.

Regardless of who pays the songwriters, the contract should clearly state what the songwriters are entitled to:

> *The royalties payable to the composer(s) of any Composition here-under pursuant to any songwriter agreement as aforesaid shall not exceed (or, in the event no songwriter agreement shall exist, shall be) the following: the writer's share [one-half (1/2) of all net sums actually received in the United States] (less any costs for collection) specifically allocable to any such Composition for mechanical rights, print rights, synchronization rights, and for any other use or exploitation of such Composition anywhere in the world. The compensation specified here-inabove shall be payable solely to any such composer in instances where such composer is the sole author of any such entire Composition, including the words and music thereof. However, in the event that one or more other songwriters, including writers of lyrics to any such Composition, are authors along with such composer on any such Composition, then the compensation specified in the immediately pre-ceding subparagraph shall be divided and paid in equal shares to each such author of any such Composition, unless the composers thereof shall otherwise agree in writing.*

Fifty percent of the net receipts is the writer's share of the income and, accordingly, the amount that most agreements will limit payments to. Should a publisher, for some reason, agree to pay a songwriter more than half of the receipts, the administrator should not be penalized for that decision. Therefore, this clause would set the writer's share to half, then the publisher would have to pay any additional amounts due out of its portion of the proceeds. Of course, if there is more than one writer, all writers would have to split the fifty percent amongst themselves.

D. Warranties

As with other contracts we have discussed, the publisher will have to make promises to the administrator in order to protect the administrator and ensure the administrator that it is getting what it bargains for. This includes giving the administrator the benefit of any promises made to the publisher by the songwriter.

> *Each party hereto gives the other the equal benefits of any warranties that it has obtained or shall obtain under any agreement affecting the Compositions, including songwriters' contracts. Publisher further represents and warrants that (i) the exercise by Administrator of any of the rights granted hereunder will not violate or infringe upon any common law or statutory rights of any third party, including, without limitation, contractual rights, copyrights and rights of privacy; (ii) it presently does, and during the term hereof shall, maintain exclusive, valid songwriters' contracts with any composers who may write or co-write any Compositions hereunder which are published by Publisher and that it shall not breach said contracts or permit any breach thereof; and (iii) it has not heretofore accepted nor will it during the term hereof accept an advance of publishing royalties from its record company or from any other party without Administrator's consent. With respect to any composer who may write or co-write any Composition hereunder, Administrator shall have the right to use the name and likeness of any such composer for advertising and purposes of trade in connection with the exploitation of the applicable Composition(s).*

This clause demonstrates the standard promises. The publisher has to promise that the compositions do not infringe anyone else's copyright (as we have discussed, to protect against lawsuits and provide a recourse if a lawsuit should occur); that it has gotten contracts from the songwriters (to ensure that the songwriter has actually assigned publishing to this particular publisher); and that the publisher has not accepted an advance of publishing royalties (which would mean that the publisher has already accepted money for licenses that the administrator would have to manage and no earnings would be forthcoming). The administrator must also ensure that the publisher has the right to use any co-writer's name and picture for promoting the song.

E. Indemnities

As you might suspect, where there are promises, there will be indemnities and the right to withhold royalties.

> *Publisher indemnifies and holds Administrator, its assigns, licensees and its and their directors, officers, shareholders, agents and employees harmless from any liability, including, without limitation, reasonable counsel fees and court costs, arising out of or connected with or resulting from any claim inconsistent with any of the warranties, representations or agreements, express or implied, and made by Publisher in this agreement. Administrator shall give Publisher prompt written notice of any claim or action covered by said indemnity, and Administrator shall have the right to withhold payment of any and all monies hereunder in reasonable amounts related to such claim or action pending the disposition thereof. All of such withheld monies shall be deposited in an interest bearing account in a federally insured bank or savings and loan association, and shall be distributed upon a settlement or final judgment of any such claim or action in accordance with the rights of parties thereto.*

F. Copyright prosecution

Although the administrator does not own any of the copyrights in the compositions, it may still reserve the right to protect the copyrights from infringements by others. The administrator derives income from the composition and, therefore, has an interest in making sure that it is not used by those without any rights to it.

> *Administrator shall have the right but not the obligation to prosecute, defend and settle all claims and actions with respect to the Compositions and the copyrights or other rights with respect to the Compositions; provided, however, Administrator shall not settle claims or actions without the consent of Publisher. In the event of a recovery by Administrator or Publisher of any monies as a result of a judgment or settlement, such monies shall be divided between Administrator and Publisher in the same shares as provided in paragraph 3 above, after first deducting the expenses of obtaining said monies, including reasonable counsel fees. Publisher shall have the right to provide counsel for itself, to assist in or assume the prosecution or defense of any such*

matter, but at its own expense. Any judgments against Administrator and any settlements by Administrator of claims against it respecting any of the Compositions, together with costs and expenses, including counsel fees, shall be subject to the indemnity provisions of paragraph 5 hereof, and Publisher's indemnity payments thereunder shall be paid to Administrator from any and all sums that may become due to Publisher hereunder, or promptly upon demand by Administrator.

G. Accountings

The administrator must give accountings, and pay out royalties that are due, on a regular basis. Furthermore, the agreement should outline the audit procedures and establish a period within which a statement may be contested before it is binding.

Statements as to all monies payable hereunder shall be sent by Administrator to Publisher within sixty (60) days after the end of each calendar quarter for each such preceding quarterly period. Publisher shall be deemed to have consented to all royalty statements and other accounts rendered by Administrator to it, and said statements and other accounts shall be binding upon Publisher and not subject to any objection for any reason, unless specific objection in writing, setting forth the basis thereof, is given by Publisher to Administrator within two (2) years from the date rendered. A Certified Public Accountant, on Publisher's behalf, at reasonable intervals, may examine the books of Administrator pertaining to the Compositions, during Administrator's usual business hours and upon prior reasonable notice. Said books relating to activities and receipts may be examined during the two (2) years period following delivery by Administrator of the statement for said accounting period.

H. Term

Unlike the transfer of publishing, which is permanent, an administration agreement has a discreet term:

The initial term of this agreement shall be three (3) years from the date of execution hereof by both parties as set forth below, and unless written notice of the termination of this agreement shall have been sent by either party hereto to the other at least sixty (60) days prior to the expiration of the initial term, then this agreement shall be renewed upon a year to year basis, and Publisher, or Administrator, shall be required to give notice as aforesaid for any termination of any such renewal period. If any such notice shall be so given, then any such termination shall be effective on the first day of the calendar quarter next following the expiration of the initial term or renewal period, as applicable. Notwithstanding the foregoing, no such notice of termination shall be deemed effective unless, prior to the date upon which this agreement is to terminate, Administrator shall have recouped or been paid by Publisher its reasonable expenses (as said term is defined herein) theretofore incurred.

Three to five years is a fairly common range for the term. Here, the contract provides for an automatic year-to-year extension unless one of the companies ends the agreement with a sixty-day notice. You should note that the agreement cannot be terminated until the administrator has recouped any expenses and advances it may have incurred.

The agreement should also provide for situations where a license extends beyond the term of the agreement.

When Administrator shall license any right or assume the collection obligations of an existing license to one (1) or more of the Compositions, the terms of this agreement in respect to that license shall extend until (i) three (3) years after the issuance of said license, or (ii) the termination of the overall agreement, whichever is later.

For example, let's say our publisher, Uptown, has an administration agreement with Sky's the Limit Publishing that lasts for three years. One year before the agreement expires, Uptown negotiates and issues a license to an unrelated company that lasts for three years. Since Uptown did the work, it will want to ensure that it gets the full benefit of the income that it bargained for under its agreement. For that single license, Uptown will continue to administer for three years, even though its rights under its agreement with Sky's the Limit will expire one year after the license is issued.

The administrator would also want some incentive for securing cover recordings of the compositions:

c. *When Administrator shall secure any cover recording of a Composition hereunder the term of this agreement with respect to any such Composition shall thereafter extend in perpetuity.*

As discussed in earlier chapters, cover recordings are a valuable source of income for the songwriter and publisher. Because the administrator's efforts have resulted in the cover recording, which is a permanent source of income for the publisher, the administrator will want to share in that source for its duration. Therefore, although the administrator's rights will terminate, its rights to payment for any cover recordings it has secured will continue indefinitely.

I. Subpublishing

A subpublishing arrangement is one in which an administrator (or publisher, for that matter) licenses the composition to another publisher in another country, so that the second publisher can administer the composition within that country. Subpublishing arrangements are very common, both with subsidiary companies and with independent companies. Therefore, if the administrator is to be responsible for collecting all income, worldwide, generated by the song, then the administrator must reserve the right to issue licenses to subpublishers:

> Administrator may enter into subpublishing or collection agreements with and license or assign this agreement and any of its rights hereunder and delegate any of its obligations hereunder to third parties throughout the world. In the event Administrator is or shall be a party to any subpublishing, collection or administration agreement for any country of the world with a subsidiary or affiliate of Administrator, such agreement shall be deemed to be an agreement with an unrelated third party.

Conclusion

Because of the importance of publishing income, it is essential that the compositions be correctly documented and administered. Usually, the record company and its publishing company simply have the better resources to see to it that this is done. This is especially true considering that many songwriters are also performers that spend a lot of time on stage and very little time attending to business functions. Therefore, an independent record label with a publishing company that can step in and take over stands to increase the profitability of the song and, ultimately, the record company's bottom line.

Forms
Administration Agreement

THIS AGREEMENT is made as of_____, 200__, by and between Uptown Music, Inc. (hereinafter referred to as "Administrator") and Sky's the Limit Publishing (hereinafter sometimes referred to, individually and collectively, as "Publisher").

1. This agreement is made with respect to all musical compositions, heretofore or during the term hereof, written or composed, in whole or in part, or owned or controlled, directly or indirectly, by Publisher or any firm or corporation affiliated with or related to it or which it shall form, a complete schedule of which, as of the date hereof, is set forth on Schedule "A" attached hereto (such musical compositions being hereinafter referred to as the "Compositions"). During the term hereof, Administrator shall have the exclusive right to administer and exploit the Compositions throughout the world; to print, publish, sell, use and license the performance and use of the Compositions throughout the world; and to execute in Publisher's name any licenses and agreements affecting the Compositions, including, but not limited to, licenses for mechanical reproduction, public performance and synchronization uses, and to assign in the normal course of business or license all such rights to third parties. Administrator in its discretion or at the request of Publisher, and on receipt of all necessary information, shall register in the name of Publisher claims to copyright in the Compositions together with any other documents which Administrator deems necessary to register in the United States Copyright Office.

2. Administrator shall collect all gross receipts earned by and derived from the Compositions during the term hereof, regardless of when paid. "Gross receipts" is defined as any revenue derived from the Compositions less amounts paid to or deducted by foreign subpublishers, sublicensees, collection agencies and local performing and mechanical rights societies. Gross receipts shall include, without limitation, mechanical royalties, synchronization fees, print income and the "writer's" and "publisher's share" of public performance income, provided, however, that the composers of any Compositions hereunder shall have the right to collect the "writer's

share" of any such income directly from the applicable performing rights society.

3. a. For its services hereunder, Administrator shall be paid its reasonable expenses as set forth in subparagraphs (b)(i) and (ii) below, plus ten percent (10%) of the gross receipts derived from the Compositions; provided, however, that Administrator shall be entitled to twenty-five percent (25%) of the gross receipts derived from cover recordings of the Compositions secured by Administrator. The term "cover recording" shall mean any recording of a Composition by any person other than the composer or composers of such Composition, or placement of a Composition in a motion picture, television pro9ram or commercial. In the event there shall be both cover records and other records released of any Composition hereunder, then, for the purposes of the computation of Administrator's fees, performance income with respect to any such Composition shall be divided into two (2) categories in the same proportion that mechanical income is earned during the period that any such performance income is earned, and the applicable percentages hereunder paid with respect to any such mechanical income shall be paid with respect to each such category of performance income.

    b. "Reasonable expenses" are defined as the following: (i) actual out-of-pocket non-overhead administrative and exploitation expenses of Administrator with respect to the Compositions including, without limitation, registration fees, the costs of transcribing for lead sheets, and the costs of producing demonstration records to the extent such expenses are not recouped from the composer's royalties; provided, however Administrator shall incur no single expense in excess of Fifty Dollars ($50) without the consent of Publisher; and (ii) attorneys' fees, if any, actually paid by Administrator for any agreements (other than the present agreement) affecting the Compositions.

    c. Songwriter royalties shall be paid to any composer (including Publisher, if applicable) of any Composition hereunder. Said royalties shall be paid pursuant to any songwriter agreement between any such composer and Publisher or Publisher's predecessor in interest, if any, and such accounting to any such composer (other than Publisher, if applicable) shall be on a semi-annual basis unless required otherwise by such agreement. True copies of any such agreement shall be promptly submitted by Publisher to Administrator. Administrator shall have the election of paying on Publisher's behalf any such composer such royalties or paying such royalties to Publisher, in trust, for payment over by Publisher to any such composer. The royalties payable to the composer(s) of any Composition hereunder pursuant to any songwriter agreement as aforesaid shall not exceed (or, in the event no songwriter agreement shall exist, shall be) the following: the writer's share [one-half (1/2) of all net sums actually received in the United States] (less any costs for collection) specifically allocable to any such Composition for mechanical rights, print rights, synchronization rights, and for any other use or exploitation of such Composition anywhere in the world. The compensation specified hereinabove shall be payable solely to any such composer in instances where such composer is the sole author of any such entire Composition, including the words and music thereof. However, in the event that one or more other songwriters, including writers of lyrics to any such Composition, are authors along with such composer on any such Composition, then the compensation specified in the immediately preceding subparagraph shall be divided and paid in equal shares to each such author of any such Composition, unless the composers thereof shall otherwise agree in writing.

4.   Each party hereto gives the other the equal benefits of any warranties which it has obtained or shall obtain under any agreement affecting the Compositions, including songwriters' contracts. Publisher further represents and warrants that (i) the exercise by Administrator of any of the rights granted hereunder will not violate or infringe upon any common law or statutory rights of any third party, including, without limitation, contractual rights, copyrights and rights of privacy; (ii) it presently does, and during the term hereof shall, maintain exclusive, valid songwriters' contracts with any composers who may write or co-write any Compositions hereunder which are published by Publisher and that it shall not breach said contracts or permit any breach thereof; and (iii) it has not heretofore accepted nor will it during the term hereof accept an advance of publishing royalties from its record company or from any other party without Administrator's consent. With respect to any composer who may write or co-write any Composition hereunder, Administrator shall have the right to use the name and likeness of any such composer for advertising and purposes of trade in connection with the exploitation of the applicable Composition(s).

5. Publisher indemnifies and holds Administrator, its assigns, licensees and its and their directors, officers, shareholders, agents and employees harmless from any liability, including, without limitation, reasonable counsel fees and court costs, arising out of or connected with or resulting from any claim inconsistent with any of the warranties, representations or agreements, express or implied, and made by Publisher in this agreement. Administrator shall give Publisher prompt written notice of any claim or action covered by said indemnity, and Administrator shall have the right to withhold payment of any and all monies hereunder in reasonable amounts related to such claim or action pending the disposition thereof. All of such withheld monies shall be deposited in an interest bearing account in a federally insured bank or savings and loan association, and shall be distributed upon a settlement or final judgment of any such claim or action in accordance with the rights of parties thereto.

6. Administrator shall have the right but not the obligation to prosecute, defend and settle all claims and actions with respect to the Compositions and the copyrights or other rights with respect to the Compositions; provided, however, Administrator shall not settle claims or actions without the consent of Publisher. In the event of a recovery by Administrator or Publisher of any monies as a result of a judgment or settlement, such monies shall be divided between Administrator and Publisher in the same shares as provided in paragraph 3 above, after first deducting the expenses of obtaining said monies, including reasonable counsel fees. Publisher shall have the right to provide counsel for itself, to assist in or assume the prosecution or defense of any such matter, but at its own expense. Any judgments against Administrator and any settlements by Administrator of claims against it respecting any of the Compositions, together with costs and expenses, including counsel fees, shall be subject to the indemnity provisions of paragraph 5 hereof, and Publisher's indemnity payments thereunder shall be paid to Administrator from any and all sums that may become due to Publisher hereunder, or promptly upon demand by Administrator.

7. Statements as to all monies payable hereunder shall be sent by Administrator to Publisher within sixty (60) days after the end of each calendar quarter for each such preceding quarterly period. Publisher shall be deemed to have consented to all royalty statements and other accounts rendered by Administrator to it, and said statements and other accounts shall be binding upon Publisher and not subject to any objection for any

reason, unless specific objection in writing, setting forth the basis thereof, is given by Publisher to Administrator within two (2) years from the date rendered. A Certified Public Accountant, on Publisher's behalf, at reasonable intervals, may examine the books of Administrator pertaining to the Compositions, during Administrator's usual business hours and upon prior reasonable notice. Said books relating to activities and receipts may be examined during the two (2) years period following delivery by Administrator of the statement for said accounting period.

8.   a.   The initial term of this agreement shall be three (3) years from the date of execution hereof by both parties as set forth below, and unless written notice of the termination of this agreement shall have been sent by either party hereto to the other at least sixty (60) days prior to the expiration of the initial term, then this agreement shall be renewed upon a year to year basis, and Publisher, or Administrator, shall be required to give notice as aforesaid for any termination of any such renewal period. If any such notice shall be so given, then any such termination shall be effective on the first day of the calendar quarter next following the expiration of the initial term or renewal period, as applicable. Notwithstanding the foregoing, no such notice of termination shall be deemed effective unless, prior to the date upon which this agreement is to terminate, Administrator shall have recouped or been paid by Publisher its reasonable expenses (as said term is defined herein) theretofore incurred.

       b.   When Administrator shall license any right or assume the collection obligations of an existing license to one (1) or more of the Compositions, the terms of this agreement in respect to that license shall extend until (i) three (3) years after the issuance of said license, or (ii) the termination of the overall agreement, whichever is later.

       c.   When Administrator shall secure any cover recording of a Composition hereunder the term of this agreement with respect to any such Composition shall thereafter extend in perpetuity.

9.   The respective addresses of Administrator and Publisher for all purposes of this agreement shall be as set forth below, until written notice of a new address shall be duly given:

Administrator: Publisher:

All notices shall be in writing and shall either be delivered by registered or certified mail, postage prepaid, or by telegraph or facsimile, all charges prepaid. Neither party shall be deemed to be in breach of any of its obligations hereunder unless and until the party claiming a breach shall have given the other written notice by certified or registered mail, return receipt requested, specifying the nature of such breach and such other party shall have failed to cure such breach within thirty (30) days after receipt of such written notice; provided that if the alleged breach is of such a nature that it cannot be completely cured within thirty (30) days, the notified party shall not be deemed to be in breach if such party commences the curing thereof with due diligence within a reasonable time thereafter.

10. Administrator may enter into subpublishing or collection agreements with, and license or assign this agreement and any of its rights hereunder and delegate any of its obligations hereunder to third parties throughout the world. In the event Administrator is or shall be a party to any subpublishing, collection or administration agreement for any country of the world with a subsidiary or affiliate of Administrator, such agreement shall be deemed to be an agreement with an unrelated third party.

11. Each party acknowledges and represents that, in executing this Agreement it has received advice as to its legal rights from legal counsel and that the person signing on its behalf has read and understood all of the terms and provisions of this Agreement. Further, each party and their counsel have cooperated in the drafting and preparation of this Agreement. It shall be deemed their joint work product and may not be construed against any party by reason of its preparation or word processing.

12. This agreement sets forth the entire understanding between the parties, and cannot be modified, terminated or rescinded except by mutual written agreement of both parties hereto. This agreement shall be governed and construed under the laws of the State of _____ applicable to agreements made and wholly performed therein.

IN WITNESS WHEREOF, the parties have caused this agreement to be executed as of the day and year first set forth above.

PART THREE

OTHER AGREEMENTS

Chapter 6

Licensing Made Easy...Sort Of

One of the most important aspects of the music business is licensing. Once a composition is created, it belongs to the songwriter (or publisher). That means that no one else may use the composition in any way without the owner's permission. The license is permission to do something with the song, whether that something is to record it, perform it, write a variation of it, print it in a magazine, or create a music video for it.

There are numerous licenses used by record companies. The following are the most common, but are not intended to be an exhaustive list. For instance, you will notice that we discussed performing the song, but there is no coverage of any performance licenses. That is because performance licenses are most commonly issued by ASCAP, SESAC, or BMI, rather than by the individual songwriter or publisher. As we discussed in chapter 2, ASCAP, BMI and SESAC are the companies that are responsible for collecting and distributing performance royalties that result from radio play, live performances, jukebox performances, television performances, etc. Therefore, because the royalty collection societies are largely responsible for those licenses, we will not address them here.

There are other licensing issues to consider, as well. One of the more complicated matters to consider is the licensing of a sound recording. Although the underlying song is owned by the songwriter (and publisher), the actual recording itself belongs to the record company. Therefore, if someone wants to use the sound recording for any reason, then he or she must request permission from both the publisher and the record company. We'll discuss this in a little more depth below.

For now, be aware that different uses require different licenses. Licenses can be simple or elaborate, broad or narrow in scope, formal or informal. Regardless of the type of license you are dealing with, however, if the license does not give the person requesting it a given right, then that right is reserved by the owner. Therefore, if the person requesting the license wants to be sure he or she has the right to do something, the license should spell that out.

Mechanical Licenses

A mechanical license agreement is permission given by a publisher to a record company to mechanically reproduce and distribute a composition. Put simply, this is a license that the record company needs from the publisher to record and release a song on an album. The copyright laws of the United States allow any person or company to mechanically reproduce a composition that has been previously published, as long as they follow the proper procedure for getting a license. Therefore, if the parties cannot negotiate a license that is agreeable to both sides, the record company can follow the procedures set forth in the laws and get a license anyway—the publisher cannot prevent the record company from recording the song.

A mechanical license will include several basic pieces of information, such as the title of the song, the writers and the publishers and the name of the recording artist:

DATE:	*July 1, 2002*
TITLE:	*Down Trodd'n*
WRITER(S):	*Fred*
	Bob
	Joe
PUBLISHER(S):	*Sky's the Limit Publishing*
	Uptown Publishing
PROJECT NO.	*Livin' Large1001 (Up All Night)*
ARTIST:	*Honkey Tonk Special*
LABEL:	*Livin' Large Records*
TIMING:	*4:25*
ROYALTY RATE:	*Statutory*
RELEASE DATE:	*January 1, 2003*

A. Limitations

The license is nearly always limited to a particular use. Therefore, the agreement will state the artist, label and album title (or album catalog number) on which the song is to be included. If Livin' Large Records obtains this license for Honkey Tonk Special to record "Down Trodd'n" on their upcoming album "Up All Night," then that is the only artist and the only album for which the completed master can be used. If Livin' Large later decides to release a greatest hits album containing "Down Trodd'n," it must obtain a new license.

> *This compulsory license covers and is limited to one particular recording of said copyrighted work as performed by the artist and on the phonorecord number identified hereinabove; and this compulsory license does not supersede nor in any way affect any prior agreements now in effect respecting phonorecords of said copyrighted work*

B. Rate

The length of the recording is important, as well. As of January 1, 2005, the rate set forth in the copyright laws for mechanical licenses is $0.085 per unit sold, for songs under 5 minutes (although, as discussed in Chapter 1, a lower rate can sometimes be negotiated). However, a different rate applies to recordings that are longer than 5 minutes. That rate, as of January 1, 2005, is $0.0165 per minute (or fraction of a minute). To illustrate, a song that is 4 minutes and 30 seconds long carries a rate of $0.085. If the album sells 5,970 copies, then the record company will end up paying $507.45 to the publisher. The publisher will then divide that money with the songwriter. If, however, the recording is 6 minutes and 7 seconds, the rate will be $0.1155. If the album sells 5,970 copies, then the record company will end up paying $689.54. If the record company negotiates a lower rate (75% of statutory is fairly common), then the record company will pay 75% of those amounts.

> *For such phonorecords sold, the royalty shall be the Statutory rate in effect at the time the phonorecord is made, except as otherwise stated hereinabove;*

C. Accounting

The record company must provide a statement and royalty payments to the publisher on a regular basis, usually quarterly or semi-annually:

You shall pay royalties and account to us as Publisher(s) semi-annually within ninety (90) days after the end of each January 1 through June 30 period and July 1 through December 31 period, on the basis of phonorecords made and distributed.

D. Default

The license is only effective if the record company lives up to its end of the bargain. If the record company doesn't pay royalties as promised, then the license is terminated. The publisher must notify the record company that the payments have not been made and give the company an opportunity to fix the problem.

In the event you fail to account to us and pay royalties as herein provided for, said Publisher(s) may give written notice to you that, unless the default is remedied within 30 days of your receipt of the notice, this compulsory license will be automatically terminated. Such termination shall render either the making or the distribution, or both, of all phonorecords for which royalties have not been paid, actionable as acts of infringement under, and fully subject to the remedies provided by, the Copyright Act

E. Notice

The law allows a person or company to obtain a mechanical license by filing a notice with the U. S. copyright Office (provided that certain procedures are correctly followed). If the license is obtained in that manner, then it isn't necessary to negotiate a license with the publisher. However, that method is a lot of trouble, considering that most publishers will grant the license if you ask for it. Therefore, if you can negotiate a license with the publisher, it isn't necessary to file the license with the copyright office.

You need not serve or file the notice of intention to obtain a compulsory license required by the Copyright Act

F. Territory

Because the statutory provisions of the Copyright laws, particularly the rate, apply only in the U. S., the license will only be effective in the U.S. A different license should be obtained for each territory in which a new rate is desired.

> *This agreement is limited to the United States, its territories and possessions.*

Biz note: As long a song has been published, the publisher has no choice but to allow you to the right to record and distribute the license, as long as the request is made in the right way and as long as you pay royalties. Although you can send a notice of intent to record the song in lieu of requesting a license, there are strict statutory guidelines (relating to the timing of the notice, the timing of the royalty payments, and other things) you must abide by in order for it to be effective. You cannot get the benefit of a reduced statutory rate without permission from the publisher. Therefore, even though you have the ability to record without the signature of the publisher, considering the strict notice and compliance requirements, record companies generally rely on requesting licenses.

Videogram/Synchronization Licenses

Although a mechanical license will cover the use of the composition on an album, it will not cover the use of the composition in a music video. If, for instance, the band Honkey Tonk Special decides to record a live album containing the song "Down Trodd'n," their record company would need a mechanical license to include the song on the album. If they also wanted to release the concert footage as a video, the record company must request another license to cover the use.

A Videogram License is a license to couple music with video, then reproduce the result and distribute it to the public. A Synchronization License allows the resulting video to be broadcast on television (or in movie theaters). Therefore, to have the right to produce a video, broadcast it on television *and* create and sell copies for home use, the record company must have a Videogram license and a Synchronization license.

Biz note: A videogram license and a synchronization license are actually two separate licenses. This generally results in paying two separate licensing fees, so many independent labels will incorporate both rights into a single license. Whether a publisher will permit this depends largely on the size and stature of the publisher you are dealing with.

The Videogram/Synchronization License, unlike the mechanical license, is not provided for in the copyright laws. This means that, if the record company and publisher cannot come to agreeable terms for a license, the record company cannot make a video.

A Videogram/Synchronization License will also include the basic pieces of information necessary to identify the song:

> *The musical composition (the "Composition") covered by this License is "Down Trodd'n." The video production ("Project") covered by this License is "Honkey Tonkin' Live and Loud," a video featuring the performance of the Composition by the performing artist "Honkey Tonk Special."*

A. Territory

The license should state where the video will be offered for sale:

> *The territory ("Territory") covered by this License is the United States.*

If the record company offers the video anywhere other than the territory listed in the license, it will be in violation of the license. Therefore, you should be sure to include all potential markets. Although all markets can be included on one license, including additional markets will generally raise the fee.

B. Rights

The "rights" provision will outline exactly what rights that the record company will have to create the video.

> *Licensor hereby grants to Licensee, its successors and assigns, the non-exclusive right, license and authority to record or re-record the Composition in synchronization or timed-relation with the Project and:*

a. *to make copies of such recording and distribute such copies throughout the Territory for exhibition by cable systems, broadcasters or other entities, or by means of media having a valid performance license therefore from American Society of Composers, Authors and Publisher or Broadcast Music, Inc., as the case may be and*

b. *to cause the fixation of the Composition as part of the Picture on video cassettes, video tapes, video discs, (hereafter referred to as "Video[s]") and similar audio-visual devices intended primarily for home use and to sell, rent or otherwise distribute such Videos to the public for use in conjunction with a television-type playback system or mechanism intended for home use only.*

According to these provisions, Livin' Large can distribute copies to television and cable stations for broadcast and sell the video through retail outlets to consumers. Take care in reviewing the licenses to ensure that they include all of the rights that you need. Remember, if the license doesn't specifically give a right, then you don't have it:

> *This License does not authorize or permit any use of the Composition not expressly set forth herein and does not include the right to alter the fundamental character of the music of the Composition, to use the title of the Composition as the title of the motion picture, to use the story of the Composition, to perform the Composition other than with the Picture, or to make any other use of the Composition not expressly authorized hereunder.*

C. Compensation

Much like other licenses, the fee may be either a per unit royalty, a flat fee, or both (particularly if the license covers both home video and broadcast rights).

> *In consideration for the aforementioned Video rights, the Licensee shall pay to Licensor the following royalties on the terms and conditions set forth below:*
>
> a. *Eight Cents ($0.08) for each Video unit sold and paid for;*
>
> b. *The sum of Two Hundred Dollars ($250.00), to be paid upon the execution and delivery hereof as a non-returnable, nonrecoupable "license fee" for granting the aforementioned rights.*

D. Term

A Videogram/Synchronization license is nearly always limited to a number of years or units (or both).

> *This license shall expire seven years from the date set forth herein-above and is limited to 2,500 units.*

Many independent labels are dangerously lax in maintaining sufficient records to be aware of when their licenses expire. It is important to understand that if you exceed the time or number of units noted in the license, you are technically infringing the publisher's copyright. Most publishers will consider the license effective as long as the record company continues to pay royalties, even beyond the expiration period, but relying on that possibility is not in your best interest.

E. Limitations

Depending upon the bargaining power of the record company, the agreement may contain either a limitation of liability:

> *Licensor warrants only that it has the sole legal right to grant this License and this License is given and accepted without other warranty or recourse. If said warranty shall be breached in whole or in part with respect to said Composition, Licensor's total liability shall be limited to repaying Licensee the consideration theretofore paid under this License with respect to said Composition.*

or an indemnification against liability:

> *Licensor warrants and agrees that it has the sole legal right to grant this License. Licensor shall indemnify and hold harmless Licensee from and against any and all claims, damages, liabilities, costs and expenses (including legal expenses and reasonable counsel fees) arising out of the use of the Composition in the Project. Licensor will reimburse Licensee on demand for any payment made at any time after the date hereof in respect of any liability or claim in respect of which Licensee is entitled to be indemnified. Licensor shall notify Licensee of any such claim and Licensor shall have the right, at its expense, to participate in the defense thereof.*

The difference between these two provisions is the record company's exposure. Under the limitation of liability, if there is a dispute of ownership that results in a claim against the record company, the publisher will have to repay any licensing fees and royalties but will not have to cover any other damages that the record company may incur. However, under the indemnification provision, if there is a dispute of ownership that results in a claim against the record company, the publisher must repay the record company for any damages that the record company suffers. Ownership disputes between composers can result in costs that well exceed any royalties paid to the publisher, including legal fees for defending a claim (whether or not the claim is won) and costs incurred in repackaging and reshipping product with corrected credits. Therefore, if the record company has any bargaining power whatsoever, it should insist on the indemnity (which protects the record company) rather than the limitation of liability (which protects the publisher).

Master Use Licenses

A frequent request from a record label is the right to use its version of a particular song. These requests range from advertisers wanting to include the song in a commercial to record companies wanting to include the song on a compilation album or sound track. Whatever its reasons, the company wants that particular version, rather than enlisting another artist to make a new recording.

A. Rights Granted

A tricky aspect of a master use license is that the master use license, standing alone, will *not* be sufficient to give the company asking to use the master all rights necessary to proceed.

> *Only in respect of the rights Livin' Large Records ("Livin' Large") owns or controls, and subject to the provisions hereof, Livin' Large hereby grants to you a non-exclusive license, during the Term as set forth herein, to perform, reproduce, manufacture, sell and/or distribute the Master for the sole purpose of exploiting the Project in the Territory, as set forth herein.*

As you can see, the record company is only granting a license for the rights that it has. This means that the right to use the composition contained on the master must be obtained directly from the publisher. Recall that a mechanical license is limited to the specific album that the record company originally records the master for, so whatever use that the new company wishes to put the master to is not covered under the original mechanical license and must be requested.

For instance, at the beginning of the chapter, Livin' Large Records requested the right to record a master for "Down Trodd'n" to be included on the album "Up All Night." If Acme Advertising decided that Honkey Tonk Special's version of the song would be perfect for a credit card company's television ad campaign, even if Livin' Large was willing to allow the use, their mechanical license did not include the right to use the song in television commercials. Therefore, although Livin' Large is granting Acme the right to use the sound recording, Acme must request the right to use the composition from the publisher, as well.

B. Term and Territory

As with other licenses, the master use license is usually limited to a specific territory, and a term of years/number of units:

> *The Term of this Agreement (the "Term") shall be for a period of five (5) years from January 1, 2003, and for no more than 2,500 units. The territory covered by this Agreement is limited to the United States (the "Territory").*

C. Credits

If a record company is to allow the use of its recording, it will want credit. The record company should reserve the right to review any label copy before it is finalized.

> *You shall accord Livin' Large credit, substantially as set forth below, with respect to the Master on all labels, liner notes, and outside packaging*

> *Down Trodd'n*
> *Performed by Honkey Tonk Special*
> *Courtesy of Livin' Large Records, Inc.*

You will require compliance with the foregoing credit requirements in all agreements for the performance, reproduction, manufacture, sale, distribution or other exploitation of the Project. A designated representative of Livin' Large shall be afforded an opportunity to review the label copy to ensure that the proper credit has been accorded to Livin' Large.

D. Representations and Warranties

As we discussed, the record company is granting only the right to use the sound recording, not the composition itself. Because claims of copyright violations tend to include everyone involved in the transaction, the record company should take extra care to ensure that the person requesting the right to use the master gets all of the necessary licenses and permissions before using the master.

a.   *You warrant, represent and agree that you will obtain in writing all requisite consents and permissions of labor organizations, if any, the copyright owners and the Artist whose performances are embodied in the Masters and that you will pay all re-use payments, fees, royalties and other sums required to be paid for such consents and permission, under applicable collective bargaining agreements, or otherwise in connection with your use of the Master, directly to such parties, as applicable. If Livin' Large so requires, you will obtain from said persons and deliver to Livin' Large any document Livin' Large requires to confirm that they will not look to Livin' Large for any payment in connection with the use of the Master on the Project. You will not be entitled to exercise the license granted to you herein until you have fully complied with the provisions of this clause.*

This provision also clearly designates whose responsibility it is to obtain the licenses (and pay the fees). This will help guard against unnecessary claims against the record company.

The record company, on the other hand, makes no promises whatsoever, except that it owns the recording in question:

b.   *Livin' Large warrants only that Livin' Large has the right to grant the license specified herein. You accept said license without any other warranty or representation by Livin' Large or recourse against it.*

If there is a claim involving the composition itself, then, the person requesting the right to use the master cannot look to the record company for reimbursement. For instance, returning to our example above, if Acme and the credit card company are sued by Lou, who claims that he wrote the song they are using in their advertising campaign, Acme and the credit company cannot look to the record company for assistance in paying the costs of the suit.

E. Compensation

A record company is under no obligation to grant a master use license and can demand any compensation that they deem appropriate. Therefore, especially from an independent record label's standpoint, the compensation for the use can vary.

This license is conditioned upon receipt of One Hundred (100) compact discs for Licensor's own use.

In addition to the obvious flat fee or royalty arrangement, some labels will allow the use in exchange for things such as free product or additional publicity. Use your imagination. Many entities making these requests have the same cash flow problems that independent record labels have. Some examples might include educational groups looking for background music for documentaries, charitable organizations looking for tracks for a benefit album, and nonprofit organizations looking for background music for commercials. So don't be afraid to be creative with the compensation.

F. Reservation of rights

As we have discussed, all rights not expressly granted in the license are reserved to the record company:

Livin' Large reserves exclusively to itself and its successors, licensees, and assigns all rights and uses in and to the Master, whether now or hereafter known or in existence, except the limited use expressly licensed hereunder. By way of illustration and not of limitation, the following rights are specifically reserved to Livin' Large for its own use, and may not be exercised by you:

a. *All rights of reproduction or use of the Master on phonograph records, tapes and any other types of sound reproduction, in all media, whether now or hereafter known or in existence, except such reproduction in connection with the Project.*

b. *The right to use the Master in motion pictures or other television programs.*

c. *The right to alter the Master in any way.*

This catch-all provision ensures that any right not listed is not granted, and even specifies common uses that the licensee is not entitled to.

G. Termination

The record company should provide for an automatic termination if the licensee doesn't do what the license requires:

> *The license granted herein is rescinded unless you comply with the credit requirements and obtain the consents and permissions required hereunder. Said license shall terminate forthwith upon notice to you in the event of any material breach of your obligations hereunder. Any such termination shall be without prejudice to any other remedies Livin' Large may have against you.*

If the licensee fails to obtain all proper permissions or give the record company proper credit, the record company can send a notice and rescind the license (that is, it is as though the license never existed). However, the record company is not limited to simply voiding the license. It may take whatever other action the law will allow to recover for any damages that the record company may have been caused.

H. Most Favored Nations

A most favored nations provision is fairly common in the industry, and is included in many kinds of licenses. What a most favored nations provision does is change the terms of the agreement to match any other agreement that has better terms:

If you shall license any other master recording at a license fee and/or upon terms more favorable to the licensor than we have been granted herein, then we shall also have the benefit of such more favorable terms.

For instance, let's assume that Livin' Large is granting a master use license to Compilation Records, Inc. Compilation Records is planning to obtain master use licenses from fourteen other companies, then use the fifteen masters to compile an album entitled "Hit Dance Tracks." If Livin' Large's license authorizes the use of the master in return for a royalty of $0.08 per unit sold, then Compilation obtains a similar license from Jamz Records promising a royalty of $0.10 per unit sold, then Livin' Large's royalty rate automatically jumps to $0.10 per unit.

Biz note: Most record companies that grant most favored nations status interpret this clause by reading all terms together, rather than separately. For instance, in the above example, say Livin' Large's royalty is $0.08, but they receive an advance of $500. Jamz Records' royalty is $0.10, but their advance is only $250. Compilation Records might say that Jamz Records didn't really get better terms, since their advance is half of that paid to Livin' Large, and might continue to extend the $0.08 royalty to Livin' Large, despite the most favored nations provision. Whether this is permissible or not depends largely on the wording of the specific contract at issue.

Side Artist Agreements

Frequently, a recording artist will have the opportunity to record with another artist. If each artist is signed to a different label, then someone will be in breach of a contract if the recording proceeds, unless one of the record companies waives its rights to its exclusive artist. Most record companies are willing to give a limited waiver permit the recording. There are several benefits to such an arrangement. The artist gets publicity. The record company can (and often does) request that the other artist make a guest appearance on their label in the future. Further, the record company can reserve the right to use the master on a future "greatest hits" album by their own artist, resulting in rights to a recording for which the company has incurred no cost.

Okay, so how does this work? Largely, the contract will depend on how flexible the releasing record company is willing to be. However, as with most agreements, there are several common elements.

A. Waiver of Exclusivity

The services of the recording artist are the exclusive property of the record company. Therefore, in order for another record company to use a recording on which the artist performs, there must be a waiver of those rights. Like the mechanical license, the waiver is specifically limited to the album in question. For instance, let's say More or Less Records' recording artist, Floyd, makes a special guest appearance at a Groove Therapy concert, and Livin' Large wishes to record the performance and release it as part of Groove Therapy's live album.

> *More or Less Records waives its exclusive rights to Floyd's services and consents to inclusion by Livin' Large of the Master recording of "Hang On" on the Album "Groove Therapyed Too Thin" for distribution solely by Livin' Large upon the following conditions:*

You will note that the distribution of the album is also limited to the record company. For instance, in this case, if Livin' Large wanted to sell the master recording to Dragon Records, the agreement would not apply. Dragon could not use the master without entering into its own agreement with More or Less.

Biz note: Some side artist agreements do not limit the agreement to the record company at hand. Some record companies will want the right to assign the agreement, either to sell the master or to give another company compilation rights.

B. Rights

As we discussed above, the contract must spell out exactly what rights are granted to the record company. This is the place for the record company to state its intentions.

> *Livin' Large's right to use the Master shall include the right to include the Master on the Album and the right to use the Master on singles derived from the Album.*

In this example, Livin' Large will be allowed to include the master on its album and may release the song as a single. Remember that rights that are not stated are not granted. Many side artist agreements will not allow the release of the master as a single and, therefore, the right would not be listed here. Some agreements will include the right to place the song on a greatest hits album or to release a promotional video. Again, whatever the record company plans to do with the master must be set out here.

C. Name

As we discussed in Chapter 1, one of the rights an artist grants to his or her record company as part of the recording artist agreement is the sole right to use the artists name and likeness (photo, biographical information, etc.) in connection with the sale of albums. Therefore, if the company that is making the recording wishes to have any rights at all to use the borrowed artist's name, the agreement must say that:

   a. *Livin' Large, its licensees and affiliates each will be entitled without additional payment to reproduce, use and publish Floyd's name solely for the purpose of advertising, promotion, and trade (including packaging and marketing materials) in connection with the Album, provided, however, that the name of each participating artist on the Album will also appear wherever Floyd's name appears, and Floyd's name shall be in the same size and typeface as the names of all other artists, and Floyd's name will not appear more or less prominently than any other name.*

As you can see, however, the right is not without limits. Here, Livin' Large can use the artist's name, but cannot draw attention to it. For instance, if there are other featured artists on the album, Floyd's name cannot appear without the other artists' names. Livin' Large can't print Floyd's name bigger than the other artist's name or on a sticker on the front of the album that says in large letters **"Featuring the hit song Hang On as performed by Floyd."**

Naturally, if a record company is going to allow its artist to record for another company, it will expect to receive proper credit:

   b. *Livin' Large will accord More or Less credit on the packaging of all copies of Albums embodying the Master in the following form: "Floyd appears courtesy of More or Less Records". Any failure to comply with the provisions of this paragraph shall not be a breach of this Agreement. More or Less's sole right and remedy in that event shall be to notify Livin' Large of that failure, after which Livin' Large shall use its best efforts to accord that credit to More or*

Less Records on items manufactured after Livin' Large receives that notice.

You should note that if the record company releasing the album inadvertently neglects to include the credit, that is *not* grounds for a suit. For instance, if Livin' Large's administrative department did not get the contract in its offices before the album's artwork was done, and the credit was missed because there was no paperwork to remind them to add it, all More or Less Records could do would be to report the oversight and wait for the next print run for the problem to be corrected.

As with the limitations placed on the use of the master, the record company will also place limitations on the use of its artist's name.

> c. *No use other than that set forth in herein shall be made by Livin' Large of Floyd's name.*

D. Warranties and Indemnity

Similar to other agreements in the industry, the company asking for the rights will have to make certain promises and guarantees, including an indemnity to the company that is handing over its artist:

> a. *Livin' Large warrants and represents that it shall obtain all rights and make all payments necessary for use of the Master from all third parties and More or Less shall have no liability to any person, other than payment to Floyd of royalties hereunder, in respect of any use of the Master on the Album by Livin' Large or its licensees or assigns.*
>
> b. *Livin' Large agrees to and does hereby indemnify, save and hold More or Less harmless from any and all loss and damage (including court costs and reasonable attorney's fees) arising out of any failure of, breach, or threatened breach by Livin' Large of any warranty, representation or agreement contained in this agreement.*

E. Compensation

Generally, a record company is compensated for giving up rights in its artist either by collecting royalties or by a flat fee. Depending upon the record company, the flat fee or royalty can be paid to the record company, which splits it with the artist according to the recording artist contract, or as an honorarium directly to the artist.

    a. In full consideration of More or Less's waiver of exclusivity in connection with the Master, Livin' Large agrees to pay directly to More or Less a royalty (the "More or Less Royalty") on Net Sales of Records which embody the Master which shall be equal to the greatest royalty payable to any side artist on the Album. Such royalty shall be a percentage of the artist net royalty or of the percentage of net receipts accruable and/or payable to Our Artist for the Master. The More or Less Royalty shall be payable after recoupment of recording costs actually paid for the Master at the all-in rate, i.e., the aggregate royalty rate payable by Livin' Large to all royalty participants for the Master, including More or Less. More or Less's Royalty shall be calculated and paid in the same manner and at the same times as royalties for Our Artist are calculated and paid. We shall attach as an exhibit hereto the relevant royalty and accounting provisions of our agreement for Our Artist's recording services.

Note that this provision assumes the side artist will be paid a royalty based on a percentage that is identical to the royalty received by Livin' Large's artist. Therefore, if Livin' Large pays Groove Therapy a rate of 15% under Livin' Large's contract with Groove Therapy, then Livin' Large expects to pay 15% to More or Less for Floyd's services.

However, a side artist is almost always enlisted to perform on a single track, rather than on the entire album. Therefore, if the artist is to receive royalties, those royalties must be prorated for the number of tracks that the artist actually performs on and must account for the fact that there is more than one artist appearing on the track, rather allowing the side artist to receive all artist royalties for the entire album.

    b. Notwithstanding anything to the contrary contained herein, More or Less's Royalty on the Album will be computed by multiplying the otherwise applicable royalty rate by a fraction, the numerator of which will be one (1) divided by the number of artist(s) to whom Livin' Large is obligated to pay royalties in respect of the sale of Phonograph Records derived form such Master and the denominator of which will be the total number of royalty-bearing master recordings embodied on the Album.

According to this formula, if there are 12 tracks on the album, then More or Less will receive a royalty of $(1 \div 2)/12 \times 15\%$, or $.625\%$.

F. Accounting

If there are royalties to be paid, then Livin' Large will need to render a regular accounting to More or Less, showing the sales of the album and the royalties accrued to More or Less for the accounting period. Naturally, if there is to be a flat fee (or no fee at all) for the artist's services, then no accounting is necessary.

> a. *Livin' Large will account directly to More or Less for the More or Less Royalty no less frequently than semi-annually. Livin' Large will compute the More or Less Royalty and render accountings, together with any applicable payment to More or Less, at the address set forth on page 1 above or otherwise as More or Less directs Livin' Large in writing.*

In order to ensure accuracy, whenever there is an accounting to be rendered, there must also be rights to examine the books of company making the accounting.

> b. *Livin' Large hereby grants to More or Less the right, at any time within one (1) year after Livin' Large issues any royalty statement relating to the More or Less Royalty, to examine the books and records of Livin' Large upon customary terms with respect to such statements insofar as they pertain to exploitation of the Master.*

This provision is fairly simple—More or Less can audit Livin' Large's books that relate to Floyd, provided that the examination is conducted within a year after the disputed statement is issued. More elaborate provisions may allow a specific period for a notice that an audit will be conducted, a specific period for the audit to actually be conducted, then another specific period within which any dispute may be taken to court.

G. Royalties and Permissions

More or Less will want to be sure that allowing Floyd to perform for Livin' Large will not create any further obligations for More or Less.

> *Livin' Large shall be responsible for obtaining the appropriate licenses, and for paying any royalties with respect to Master.*

This clause will place the obligation for obtaining all licenses, and paying all royalties, upon More or Less.

Work For Hire

A work for hire agreement is a simple but important arrangement that the record company makes with those who participate in the recording but are not featured on the recording, such as background singers and musicians. A work for hire agreement transfers any rights that the person might have in the recording to the record company in exchange for some set compensation, such as a flat fee or a designated number of copies of the recording.

Recall that, even when dealing with featured artists, the record company owns the resulting recording. However, featured artists are made other promises, such as recording advances, continuing royalties or the right to input concerning the final product. A work for hire arrangement promises nothing other than the compensation, and takes away any and all rights from the non-featured artist. The non-featured artists are not even promised a credit on the recording. Although the record company may credit the non-featured artists, when the background players are large groups such as choirs or orchestras, naming each individual is simply not practical. Therefore, the record company will not assume any obligation to give a credit.

Work for hire agreements are usually non-negotiable from the record company's standpoint. If a non-featured artist will not settle for what the record company offers, there are plenty of other candidates to choose from.

A. Compensation

As with other agreements, creativity is the key to compensation. For small record labels with limited resources, the compensation is usually the hardest part. However, keep in mind, almost any compensation that the non-featured artist will agree to is enough to make the agreement binding. You can promise $100, $10 or two copies of the completed compact disc.

> *I, the undersigned, do hereby acknowledge the following as the terms of my employment with Livin' Large Records, Inc. ("Livin' Large") in connection with the song entitled "Hold On" (the "Recording"). I will*

receive the sum of $500.00 as consideration for the services that I will render in connection with the Recording.

Note that "services rendered" is very general. If you try to make the services too specific (such as "in connection with my singing back up vocals on the album"), then if that person contributes anything else, it will not be covered under the work for hire agreement.

B. Ownership of final product

In essence, the person signing the work for hire agrees that he or she never has any rights in the recording in the first place. Because the record company is paying for the work, the record company owns the resulting product from the outset. However, as an added precaution, the agreement should include a safety net that will require the person to transfer any rights that may not be covered by the "work for hire" doctrine.

I understand that the work performed by me on the above referenced Recording is "work made for hire." In the event that such arrangement shall be deemed not to be a work made for hire, I hereby grant to Livin' Large all rights of every kind and nature in and to the results and proceeds of my services and performances rendered in connection with the above referenced Recording, including, without limitation, the complete, unconditional and exclusive worldwide ownership in perpetuity of the Recording. Livin' Large or its designee shall, accordingly, have the exclusive right to copyright any such Recording in Livin' Large's or its designee's name, as the sole owner and author thereof, and to secure any and all renewals and extensions of such copyrights (it being understood that for such purposes I and all persons rendering services in connection with the Recording shall be Livin' Large's employees-for-hire). Nevertheless, I shall, upon Livin' Large's request, execute and deliver to Livin' Large any assignments of copyright (including any renewals and extensions thereof) in and to the Recording as Livin' Large may deem necessary and I hereby irrevocably appoint Livin' Large, or its representative, my attorney-in-fact for the purpose of executing such assignments in my name. Without limiting any of the foregoing, Livin' Large and its designees shall have the exclusive worldwide right, in perpetuity, to exploit and deal in and with respect to the Recording; to lease, license, convey or otherwise use or dispose of the Recording by any method now or hereafter known, in any field of use; to permit the public performance thereof by radio or television broadcast, or any other method now or hereafter known, all upon such terms and conditions as Livin' Large may approve, in its sole discretion, throughout the world and to permit any other person, firm, or corporation to do any or all of the foregoing, or Livin' Large may refrain from doing any and all of the foregoing.

Notice that this agreement states that, even if the law wouldn't consider this arrangement to be a work for hire, the performer assigns all rights in the project. There are some types of projects that legally cannot be work for hire, and the assignment is necessary to cover for that contingency.

That's all there is to a work for hire agreement. Because it is so simple, there is no reason not to have one for everyone working on the project that will not receive royalties.

Conclusion

The form and content of licenses, like all other documents presented in this book, will vary, depending upon the needs and wishes of the parties involved. However, we cannot stress enough the importance of carefully documenting your agreements with some kind of writing. If the first rule of thumb is that nothing brings a lawsuit faster than a successful record, then the second is surely that if there is nothing in writing, the parties will always have a different memory of what was agreed to.

Keeping written agreements has the added bonus of helping you track your projects. Successful record companies know, at all times, how much money was spent on a project, how much in royalties will have to be paid and when, and what licenses are outstanding.

Well, that's it. This arsenal of commonly used forms, along with talented artists, proper promotion and, of course, suitable funding will set you on the path to success. Good luck!

Forms
Mechanical License

DATE:	July 1, 2002

A. TITLE: Down Trodd'n

B. WRITER(S):   Fred
                               Bob
                               Joe

    PUBLISHER(S):   Sky's the Limit Publishing
                               Uptown Publishing

C. PROJECT NO.   Livin' Large1001 (Up All Night)
    ARTIST: Honkey Tonk Special
    LABEL: Livin' Large Records
    TIMING: 4:25
    ROYALTY RATE: Statutory
    RELEASE DATE: January 1, 2004

You have advised us as the Publisher(s) referred to in (B) supra, that you wish to obtain a compulsory license to make and distribute phonorecords (including disc, 8-track, cassette and other configurations) of the copyrighted work referred to in (A) supra, under the compulsory license provision of Section 115 of the Copyright Act.

Upon doing so, you shall have all rights which are granted to, and all the obligations which are imposed upon, users of said copyrighted work under the compulsory license provision of the Copyright Act, after phonorecords of the copyrighted work have been distributed to the public in the United States under the authority of the copyright owner by another person, except that with respect to phonorecords thereof made and distributed hereunder:

1. You shall pay royalties and account to us as Publisher(s) semi-annually within ninety (90) days after the end of each January 1 through June 30 period and July 1 through December 31 period, on the basis of phonorecords made and distributed.

2. For such phonorecords sold, the royalty shall be the Statutory rate in effect at the time the phonorecord is made, except as otherwise stated in (C) supra;

3. This compulsory license covers and is limited to one particular recording of said copyrighted work as performed by the artist and on the phonorecord number identified in (C) supra; and this compulsory license does not supersede nor in any way affect any prior agreements now in effect respecting phonorecords of said copyrighted work:

4. In the event you fail to account to us and pay royalties as herein provided for, said Publisher(s) may give written notice to you that, unless the default is remedied within 30 days of your receipt of the notice, this compulsory license will be automatically terminated. Such termination shall render either the making or the distribution, or both, of all phonorecords for which royalties have not been paid, actionable as acts of infringement under, and fully subject to the remedies provided by, the Copyright Act;

5. You need not serve or file the notice of intention to obtain a compulsory license required by the Copyright Act;

6. This agreement is limited to the United States, its territories and possessions.

Videogram/Synchronization License

SYNCHRONIZATION LICENSE AGREEMENT entered into this 1st day of January, 2003, between Livin' Large Records, Inc. (hereinafter referred to as "Licensee") and Uptown Music, Inc. (hereinafter referred to as "Licensor").

1. The musical composition (the "Composition") covered by this License is Hang On.

2. The video production ("Picture") covered by this License is "Hang On," a music video featuring the performances of Groove Therapy.

3. The type of use of the Composition is limited to visual vocals no longer than five minutes in length and not used more than once in the Picture.

4. The territory ("Territory") covered by this License is the World.

5. Licensor hereby grants to Licensee, its successors and assigns, the non-exclusive right, license and authority to record or re-record the Composition in synchronization or timed-relation with the Project and: to make copies of such recording and distribute such copies throughout the Territory for exhibition by cable systems, broadcasters or other entities, or by means of media having a valid performance license therefore from American Society of Composers, Authors and Publisher or Broadcast Music, Inc., as the case may be; and to cause the fixation of the Composition as part of the Picture on video cassettes, video tapes, video discs, (hereafter referred to as "Video{s}") and similar audio-visual devices intended primarily for home use and to sell, rent or otherwise distribute such Videos to the public for use in conjunction with a television-type playback system or mechanism intended for home use only. In consideration for the aforementioned Video rights, the Licensee shall pay to Licensor the following royalties on the terms and conditions set forth below:

    a. Eight Cents ($0.08) for each Video unit sold and paid for:

    b. the sum of Five Hundred Dollars ($500.00), to be paid upon the execution and delivery hereof, receipt of which is hereby acknowledged as the "license fee" for granting the aforementioned rights and as a non-returnable advance payment recoupable only against the sale of such Videos at the royalty rate set forth above.

6. This License does not authorize or permit any use of the Composition not expressly set forth herein and does not include the right to alter the fundamental character of the music of the Composition, to use the title of the Composition as the title of the motion picture, to use the story of the Composition, or to make any other use of the Composition not expressly authorized hereunder.

7. The recording and performing rights hereinabove granted shall endure for the worldwide period of all copyrights in and to the Composition, and any and all renewals or extensions thereof that Licensor may now own or control or hereafter own or control without Licensee having to pay any additional consideration therefor.

8. Licensor warrants and agrees that it has the sole legal right to grant this License. Licensor shall indemnify and hold harmless Licensee from and against any and all claims, damages, liabilities, costs and expenses (including legal expenses and reasonable counsel fees) arising out of the use of the Composition in the Picture. Licensor will reimburse Licensee on demand for any payment made at any time after the date hereof in respect of any liability or claim in respect of which Licensee is entitled to be indemnified. Licensor shall notify Licensee of any such claim and Licensor shall have the right, at its expense, to participate in the defense thereof.

9. Licensor reserves all rights not expressly granted to Licensee hereunder. All rights granted hereunder are granted on a non-exclusive basis.

10. This License is binding upon and shall inure to the benefit of the respective successors and/or assigns of the parties hereto.

11. This License shall be governed by and subject to the laws of the State of _____ applicable to agreements made and to be wholly performed within such State.

   IN WITNESS WHEREOF, the parties have caused the foregoing to be executed as of this _____ day of _____, 200_.

Master Use License

January 1, 2003

CEO
More or Less Records
123 Main Street
Left Field, VA 12345

Dear Mr. CEO:

   The following terms and conditions shall confirm our mutual understanding and agreement regarding your use of our master recording of Hold On (the "Master") embodying the performances of Groove Therapy (the "Artist") as part of the compilation album entitled "The Best Ever Rock Hits" (the "Project").

1. Only in respect of the rights Livin' Large Records, Inc. ("Livin' Large") owns or controls, and subject to the provisions hereof, Livin' Large hereby grants to you a non-exclusive license, during the Term as set forth herein, to perform, reproduce, manufacture, sell and/or distribute the Master for the sole purpose of exploiting the Project in the Territory, as set forth herein.

2. The Term of this Agreement (the "Term") shall be for a period of five (5) years from the date set forth hereinabove. The territory covered by this Agreement is limited to the United States (the "Territory").

3. You shall accord Livin' Large credit, substantially as set forth below, with respect to the Master on all labels, liner notes, and outside packaging

    Hold On
    Performed by Groove Therapy
    Courtesy of Livin' Large Records, Inc.

    You will require compliance with the foregoing credit requirements in all agreements for the performance, reproduction, manufacture, sale, distribution or other exploitation of the Project. A designated representative of Livin' Large shall be afforded an opportunity to review the label copy to ensure that the proper credit has been accorded to Livin' Large.

4. You warrant, represent and agree that you will obtain in writing all requisite consents and permissions of labor organizations, if any, the copyright owners and the Artist whose performances are embodied in the Masters and that you will pay all re-use payments, fees, royalties and other sums required to be paid for such consents and permission, under applicable collective bargaining agreements, or otherwise in connection with your use of the Master, directly to such parties, as applicable. If Livin' Large so requires, you will obtain from said persons and deliver to Livin' Large any document Livin' Large requires to confirm that they will not look to Livin' Large for any payment in connection with the use of the Master on the Project. You will not be entitled to exercise the license granted to you herein until you have fully complied with the provisions of this clause.

5. Livin' Large warrants only that Livin' Large has the right to grant the license specified in clause 1 hereof. You accept said license without any other warranty or representation by Livin' Large or recourse against it.

6. This license is conditioned upon receipt of a non-refundable advance in the amount of $500.00.

7. Livin' Large reserves exclusively to itself and its successors, licensees, and assigns all rights and uses in and to the Master, whether now or hereafter known or in existence, except the limited use expressly licensed hereunder. By way of illustration and not of limitation, the following rights are specifically reserved to Livin' Large for its own use, and may not be exercised by you:

    a. All rights of reproduction or use of the Recording on phonograph records, tapes and any other types of sound reproduction, in all media, whether now or hereafter known or in existence, except such reproduction in connection with the Project.

    b. The right to use the Master in motion pictures or other television programs.

    c. The right to alter the Master in any way.

8. The license granted herein is rescinded unless you comply with the credit requirements of clause 3 hereof and obtain the consents and permissions required under clause 4. Said license shall terminate forthwith upon notice to you in the event of any material breach of your obligations hereunder. Any such termination shall be without prejudice to any other remedies Livin' Large may have against you.

9. The license herein granted may not be transferred or assigned by you, in whole or in part, without Livin' Large's prior written consent

10. This Agreement sets forth the entire agreement between you and Livin' Large with respect to the subject matter hereof, and no modification, amendment, waiver, termination or discharge of this Agreement or any provisions hereof shall be binding upon us unless confirmed by a written instrument signed by an officer of Livin' Large. No waiver of any provision of or default under this Agreement, shall affect Livin' Large's rights

thereafter to enforce such provision or to exercise any right or remedy in the event of any other default, whether or not similar.

11. If you shall license any other master recording at a license fee and/or upon terms more favorable to the licensor than we have been granted herein, then we shall also have the benefit of such more favorable terms.

12. The validity, construction and effect of this agreement, and any and all modifications thereof, shall be governed by the laws of the State of _____ applicable to contracts entered into and performed entirely with the State of_____.

Side Artist Agreement

January 1, 2004

CEO
More or Less Records
123 Main Street
Left Field, VA 12345

Dear Mr. CEO:

The following constitutes the agreement between Livin' Large Records ("Livin' Large") and More or Less Records ("More or Less") in respect of the use by Livin' Large of the master recording of the musical composition entitled "Hang On" (the "Master") embodying the performance of Floyd on Groove Therapy's ("Our Artist") album, Groove Therapyed Too Thin (the "Album").

1. <u>Waiver of Exclusivity</u>.

More or Less waives its exclusive rights to Floyd's services and consents to inclusion by Livin' Large of the Master on the Album for distribution solely by Livin' Large upon the following conditions:

2. <u>Rights</u>.

Livin' Large's right to use the Master shall include the right to include the Master on the Album, the right to use the Master on singles derived from the

Album, and the right to include the Master on so-called Greatest Hits albums thereafter.

3. Name.

    a.   Livin' Large, its licensees and affiliates each will be entitled without additional payment to reproduce, use and publish Floyd's name solely for the purpose of advertising, promotion, and trade (including packaging and marketing materials) in connection with the Album, provided, however, that the name of each participating artist on the Album will also appear wherever Floyd's name appears, and Floyd's name shall be in the same size and typeface as the names of all other artists, and Floyd's name will not appear more or less prominently than any other name.

    b.   Livin' Large will accord More or Less credit on the packaging of all copies of Albums embodying the Master in the following form: "Floyd appears courtesy of More or Less Records". Any failure to comply with the provisions of this paragraph shall not be a breach of this Agreement. More or Less's sole right and remedy in that event shall be to notify Livin' Large of that failure, after which Livin' Large shall use its best efforts to accord that credit to More or Less Records on items manufactured after Livin' Large receives that notice.

    c.   No use other than that set forth in subparagraph 3(a) shall be made by Livin' Large of Floyd's name.

4. Warranties and Indemnity.

    a.   Livin' Large warrants and represents that it shall obtain all rights and make all payments necessary for use of the Master from all third parties and More or Less shall have no liability to any person, other than payment to Floyd of royalties hereunder, in respect of any use of the Master on the Album by Livin' Large or its licensees or assigns.

    b.   Livin' Large agrees to and does hereby indemnify, save and hold More or Less harmless from any and all loss and damage (including court costs and reasonable attorney's fees) arising out of any failure of, breach, or threatened breach by Livin' Large of any warranty, representation or agreement contained in this agreement.

5. <u>Royalties</u>.

   a. In full consideration of More or Less's waiver of exclusivity in connection with the Master, Livin' Large agrees to pay directly to More or Less a royalty (the "More or Less Royalty") on Net Sales of Records which embody the Master which shall be equal to the greatest royalty payable to any side artist on the Album. Such royalty shall be a percentage of the artist net royalty or of the percentage of net receipts accruable and/or payable to Our Artist for the Master. The More or Less Royalty shall be payable after recoupment of recording costs actually paid for the Master at the all-in rate, i.e., the aggregate royalty rate payable by Livin' Large to all royalty participants for the Master, including More or Less. More or Less's Royalty shall be calculated and paid in the same manner and at the same times as royalties for Our Artist are calculated and paid. We shall attach as an exhibit hereto the relevant royalty and accounting provisions of our agreement for Our Artist's recording services.

   b. Notwithstanding anything to the contrary in subparagraph 5(a), More or Less's Royalty on the Album will be computed by multiplying the otherwise applicable royalty rate by a fraction, the numerator of which will be one (1) divided by the number of artist(s) to whom Livin' Large is obligated to pay royalties in respect of the sale of Phonograph Records derived form such Master and the denominator of which will be the total number of royalty-bearing master recordings embodied on the Album.

6. <u>Accounting</u>.

   a. Livin' Large will account directly to More or Less for the More or Less Royalty no less frequently than semi-annually. Livin' Large will compute the More or Less Royalty and render accountings, together with any applicable payment to More or Less, at the address set forth on page 1 above or otherwise as More or Less directs Livin' Large in writing.

   b. Livin' Large hereby grants to More or Less the right, at any time within one (1) year after Livin' Large issues any royalty statement relating to the More or Less Royalty, to examine the books and records of Livin' Large upon customary terms with respect to such statements insofar as they pertain to exploitation of the Master.

7. Mechanical Royalties.

Livin' Large shall be responsible for obtaining the appropriate licenses, and for paying mechanical royalties with respect to Livin' Large's use hereunder of the Master.

8. Definitions.

    a. "Record" means all forms of reproductions, now or hereafter known, manufactured or distributed primarily for home use, school use, juke box use, or use in means of transportation, reproducing sound alone.

    b. "Net sales" means gross sales, less returns, credits, and reserves against anticipated returns and credits.

9. Miscellaneous.

    a. This agreement contains the entire understanding of the parties relating to its subject matter. No change or termination of this agreement will be binding upon either party unless it is made by instrument signed by an officer of that party. A waiver by either party or any provision of this agreement in any instance will not be deemed to waive it for the future. All remedies, rights, undertakings, and obligations contained in this agreement will be cumulative, and none of them will be in limitation of any other remedy, right, undertaking, or obligation of either party. The captions of the paragraphs in this agreement are included for convenience only and will not affect the interpretation of any provision.

    b. More or Less may assign its rights under this agreement in whole or in part. Livin' Large shall not have the right to assign its rights or obligations hereunder without More or Less's prior written consent.

    c. Neither party will be deemed to be in breach of any of its obligations hereunder unless and until the non-breaching party has given the breaching party specific notice describing in detail the breach and the breaching party has failed to cure that breach within thirty (30) days after its receipt of that notice, or, if the breach cannot reasonably be cured within that thirty (30) day period, or it has not commenced to cure such breach within that thirty (30) day period and does not continue to cure such breach with reasonable diligence.

d. All notices to be given to Livin' Large hereunder and all statements and payments to be sent to Livin' Large hereunder will be addressed to Livin' Large at the address set forth on page 1 hereof or at such other address as Livin' Large designate by notice to More or Less. All notices to be given to Livin' Large hereunder will be addressed to Livin' Large to the attention of the President, at the address set forth on page 1 hereof or at such other address as Livin' Large designates by notice to More or Less, with a copy addressed to Legal Counsel at the same address. All notices will be in writing and will be given by personal delivery or by registered or certified mail (return receipt requested). Except as otherwise expressly provided herein, notices will be deemed given when personally delivered or mailed, except that notices of change of address will be effective only upon actual receipt.

e. The parties agree that the services to be provided herein are of a special, unique and intellectual character, which gives them peculiar value. In the event of a breach or threatened breach by either party of any of the terms or provisions of this Agreement which causes the injured party immediate, irreparable injury, both parties expressly agree that the injured party shall be entitled to injunctive relief; as permitted by law, to prevent a breach or threatened breach of this Agreement, or any portion thereof; which relief shall be in addition to any other rights or remedies, for damages or otherwise, available to either party.

Please confirm your acceptance of the foregoing by signing in the space below. Your use of the Master or any portions thereof shall constitute such acceptance.

Work For Hire

I, the undersigned, do hereby acknowledge the following as the terms of my employment with Livin' Large Records, Inc. ("Livin' Large") in connection with the song entitled "Hold On" (the "Recording"). I will receive the sum of $500.00 as consideration for the services that I will render in connection with the Recording.

I understand that the work performed by me on the above referenced Recording is "work made for hire." In the event that such arrangement shall be deemed not to be a work made for hire, I hereby grant to Livin' Large all rights of every kind and nature in and to the results and proceeds of my services and performances rendered in connection with the above referenced Recording, including, without limitation, the complete, unconditional and exclusive worldwide ownership in perpetuity of the Recording. Livin' Large or its designee shall, accordingly, have the exclusive right to copyright any such Recording in Livin' Large's or its designee's name, as the sole owner and author thereof, and to secure any and all renewals and extensions of such copyrights (it being understood that for such purposes I and all persons rendering services in connection with the Recording shall be Livin' Large's employees-for-hire). Nevertheless, I shall, upon the Livin' Large's request, execute and deliver to Livin' Large any assignments of copyright (including any renewals and extensions thereof) in and to the Recording as Livin' Large may deem necessary and I hereby irrevocably appoint Livin' Large, or its representative, my attorney-in-fact for the purpose of executing such assignments in my name. Without limiting any of the foregoing, Livin' Large and its designees shall have the exclusive worldwide right, in perpetuity, to exploit and deal in and with respect to the Recording; to lease, license, convey or otherwise use or dispose of the Recording by any method now or hereafter known, in any field of use; to permit the public performance thereof by radio or television broadcast, or any other method now or hereafter known, all upon such terms and conditions as Livin' Large may approve, in its sole discretion, throughout the world and to permit any other person, firm, or corporation to do any or all of the foregoing, or Livin' Large may refrain from doing any and all of the foregoing.

978-0-595-31129-3
0-595-31129-6

Printed in the United Kingdom
by Lightning Source UK Ltd.
129198UK00001B/66/A